JU-JITSU

JU-JITSU

Classical and Modern

Eddie Ferrie

The Crowood Press

First published in 1990 by
The Crowood Press Ltd
Ramsbury, Marlborough
Wiltshire SN8 2HR

www.crowood.com

This impression 2002

British Library Cataloguing-in-Publication Data

A catalogue record for this book is available from the British Library

ISBN 1 85223 722 8

Line-drawings by Jan Sparrow.

Acknowledgements
I am grateful to my parents, Eddie and Elsie, for their tireless support and help
over the years. Thanks also to Errol Field, both technician and teacher, for
demonstrating the techniques, and his students John and Mack for all their hard
work in the photo sessions.

Typeset by Acuté, Stroud, Glos.
Printed in Great Britain by Bookcraft (Bath) Ltd

Contents

Introduction

Writing a book about any martial art is something of a challenge, but in the case of ju-jitsu it is particularly daunting because the word ju-jitsu is a generic term for an almost undefinable system of fighting, primarily unarmed, but in some instances using weapons, which has descended to us over many centuries and across several continents. Originating in Japan, the techniques of ju-jitsu – many of which had existed for centuries before the term was coined – are generally considered to have been organised into an identifiable system by Hisamori Takenouchi, founder of the Takenouchi *Ryu* (school) in 1532. This school of martial arts tends to be regarded as the first homogeneous source of ju-jitsu techniques. However, there were many other different *ryu* practising numerous specialised systems of combat and which emphasised different elements of the art. Ju-jitsu therefore came to include techniques of punching, kicking, striking, throwing, holding, locking, choking and tying as well as the use of certain weapons.

As a name for a system of combat, ju-jitsu tells the practitioner very little. The meaning of the term is not often debated. The character *jutsu* means method or art, while the first character *ju* is usually translated as gentleness, pliability or flexibility. This could equally describe the practice of yoga, but the central axiom of the system is more revealing. The techniques of ju-jitsu were based on abstract Taoist philosophical concepts which had originated in China. Indeed, the best known

Fig 1   The kanji *for ju-jitsu, denoting flexibility of response.*

7

maxim of the ju-jitsu *ryu* was *ju yoku go o sei suru* which means 'flexibility masters hardness' and was expanded to 'softness can overcome hardness' and 'in yielding there is strength'. This is the basic principle underlying all ju-jitsu techniques; force should not be directly opposed, but rather given way to and redirected.

The range of techniques which the system comprises is vast and to describe them in full could easily take ten volumes the size of this one. The aim in writing this book, however, is to give the reader an idea of the modern form of the art as it is practised today, as well as an understanding of how and why it originated. Although the book contains many basic as well as advanced techniques it is by no means an exhaustive catalogue of the techniques of ju-jitsu, for while the techniques of the system are finite it seems that the possibilities of combination and recombination may not be. Given the limitations of space, rather than try to present just the basic beginner's techniques or only those normally described as advanced or esoteric (and by erroneous implication more effective), the aim of this book is to give a broad view of the range of the activity. A complete modern ju-jitsu book would take many hundreds of photographs and pages of text as a consequence of the vast number of subtle variations possible on basic themes.

A major problem with modern ju-jitsu is the difficulty of separating the martial aspects from the artistic elements of the system. Applying the criteria of 'combat effectiveness' there are many techniques practised in clubs and shown in demonstrations which are clearly too elaborate and complicated to be effective. Some can only be described as far-fetched. However, the instructors that teach such techniques insist that they help students develop concentration, technique and co-ordination and are justifiable for aesthetic reasons. Many of these instructors recognise that they may not be appropriate for purposes of self-defence but continue to teach them to keep their students' interest. Such cosmetic techniques can perhaps be justified as marketing strategy for attracting a gullible public and as aerobic exercise, but really have little other value and will not be found in this book.

The techniques presented here are all practical and effective ju-jitsu and could, without exception, be applied usefully in self-defence, although of course individual preferences will tend to determine which techniques a given individual might use. So far as weapons training is concerned, while it is an interesting and valid area of ju-jitsu practice, I have limited myself, for practical reasons, to defences against rather than the use of weapons.

1 Ju-jitsu: Genesis and Rebirth

Those thinking of taking up a martial art or a combat sport for the purposes of fitness and self-defence are often confused as to what exactly are the differences between judo and ju-jitsu. A similar confusion exists regarding aikido and any would-be martial artist cannot fail to recognise that although they differ in some respects these activities also have discernible common elements. The reason for this is that both judo and aikido derive to a very large extent from classical ju-jitsu. Karate, too, shares many common elements with ju-jitsu and while not directly derived from it (coming rather from Okinawa) it has many identical techniques.

The classical ju-jitsu *ryu* were the ancestors of the modern Japanese weaponless martial arts schools, but it would be misleading to think that ju-jitsu was ever a clearly defined homogeneous activity in its own right. Many of the techniques of ju-jitsu existed within other older combat systems prior to the coining of the term ju-jitsu.

The inherent confusion in the situation is made even greater because of the existence of two distinct types of ju-jitsu: classical and modern. Classical ju-jitsu is a very different phenomenon to the modern variety. Surviving classical ju-jitsu schools are very few in number, all in Japan and all teaching the techniques in the traditional way. Practitioners of classical ju-jitsu in modern Japan are regarded by their society in much the same way as English medievalists who dress in armour and joust; as entertaining eccentrics. In reality traditional ju-jitsu in Japan as a living, developing activity has been almost completely replaced by judo.

Modern ju-jitsu, on the other hand, is almost exclusively a western phenomenon and is practised by thousands in different clubs and organisations throughout Europe and America. In common with classical ju-jitsu, it, too, is anything but homogeneous. Different styles and associations have their own philosophies and emphases, ranging from the highly aesthetic (and sometimes functional) to the purely practical. Some dojo train in the use of weapons (as opposed to the study and practice of unarmed techniques against armed attacks), others market their systems as 'all-in', but unarmed fighting. Some schools teach reactive defensive philosophies while others advocate 'getting in first', taking as their motto 'do unto others as they would do unto you, but do it first'. Some exponents do not even regard ju-jitsu as a martial art and prefer to regard it as pure self-defence, leaving aside all ethical considerations.

AIKIDO AND JU-JITSU

In many respects aikido is the martial art which has the most in common and is closest in form to ju-jitsu. Aikido was founded by Morihei Ueshiba in 1942, although he first rationalised his own system of aiki-jutsu about 1925. Ueshiba *sensei* was a shinto mystic who spent his youth almost like a modern day *ronin*

Fig 2 A throw from a bent-arm lock.

(wandering samurai), travelling the length and breadth of Japan training under as many different masters in as many martial arts as he could. He studied and practised over two hundred martial art forms, concentrating mainly on Daito *Ryu* ju-jitsu, Yagyu ken-jutsu and Hozoin so-jutsu. Various forms of aiki-jutsu had existed for centuries but Ueshiba *sensei*, dissatisfied with the lack of ethical and spiritual values he perceived in the martial arts at that time, founded his own way, that of aikido, through which he sought to perfect himself.

The highly ethical and moral nature of Ueshiba aikido is reflected by the lack of violent striking techniques intended to damage an assailant. The aim of aikido was to develop a self-defence system which while protecting the user would not kill or maim the attacker. Consequently many of the more violent *atemi-waza* of the older aiki-jutsu systems were discarded. While not quite embodying the notion of turning the other cheek, aikido is extremely attractive to Christians and Buddhists alike as an essentially non-violent self-defence system. Unfortunately, it takes many years of practice to reach even the most mundane level of competence and its exalted spirituality, in practical self-defence terms, is an extreme handicap. There are two other major styles of aikido which have slightly different emphases. Yoshinkan aikido has a more realistic self-defence orientation and Tomiki aikido is characterised by a highly developed sportive form including *randori* and *shiai* knife defences.

JU-JITSU AND JUDO

Judo players often tend to have the attitude that judo is a higher form of ju-jitsu because of the successes of Kano's early Kodokan (literally 'the school for studying the way') members in tournaments against other ju-jitsu schools. However, many of the Kodokan's original members were in fact ju-jitsu experts who had been guided by Jigoro Kano into adopting a synthetic approach to training and so had pooled their skills. The great difference between Kodokan judo and the other ju-jitsu schools was that Kano had developed a type of freestyle combat called *randori*, whereas the old ju-jitsu schools trained almost entirely by practising *kata*. In a match held in Tokyo in 1885 under the auspices of the Tokyo Metropolitan Police, a team of experts from the Kodokan took on a team from the Totsuka Yoshin *Ryu*, the strongest ju-jitsu school in Japan at the time.

The match was a triumph for Kano's freestyle *randori* methodology as opposed to the traditional *kata* training: the Kodokan men completely outfought their opponents. Each team had fifteen men who were hand-picked for their combat skills. Particularly notable was the success of Saigo Shiro who completely overwhelmed his opponents with his *yama-arashi* (mountain-storm) throw. Interestingly, Saigo had learned this technique while a student of the Daito *Ryu*, an aiki-jutsu school. The Kodokan lost only two contests and drew one, thereby establishing themselves at that time as the main force in Japanese ju-jitsu.

When he devised his system of Kodokan judo, Jigoro Kano knew just what he was doing, but it should never be forgotten that Kodokan judo was derived directly from classical ju-jitsu. Kano himself trained in the Tenjin Shin'yo *Ryu* and the Kito *Ryu* and it was from these classical ju-jitsu schools that the bulk of the techniques of modern judo was culled.

11

Fig 3 Mu-ga-mu-cho; kanji *expressing the concept of selfless and total immersion in the training process of ju-jitsu.*

In the late nineteenth century classical ju-jitsu had very much fallen into disrepute and many of its exponents occupied positions of very low status in Japanese society. Unable to earn a living from teaching their craft many would emulate the boxing booths of the western world and take on all-comers for the entertainment of a fee-paying audience. Others worked as debt-collectors and 'enforcers' for the *yakuza* (Japanese underworld) or as oriental minders in drinking clubs and brothels where their job was to deal with drunks and awkward customers. Kano, however, perceived much of value in ju-jitsu both in terms of its practical worth as a method of essentially unarmed self-defence and as a cultural artefact capable of embodying traditional values. Its main drawback was the poor image – both of it and its practitioners – and it was to fall to Kano to transform that image.

In the United Kingdom judo is currently practised almost exclusively as an Olympic sport. The majority of those who participate do so with a view to improving their performance in *randori*, where they attempt to throw, hold, strangle and arm-lock training partners who attempt to do the same to them. This method of practising simulates most effectively the conditions of contest and so is appropriate as preparation for the sport of judo. Kano, however, conceived his judo to be much more than a mere sport. It has often been said that in typical Japanese eclectic fashion he took what was best from the numerous ju-jitsu *ryu* to create his own more practicable system which he named judo. This is, essentially, true but in fact he did much more than that. Of special significance was his choice of the characters *ju* and *do* which were to form the name of his new system. The first character, *ju* denotes flexibility and hints at the ability of softness to overcome hardness – one of the concepts intrinsic to ju-jitsu from its inception. There is nothing particularly innovative in that, but combined with the second character, *do* denoting way, or spiritual path, the combat system that was ju-jitsu became raised to a different level.

The beginner going to watch classes training in each system would immediately notice the difference in emphasis between the judo dojo and the ju-jitsu dojo. To the untrained eye the judo dojo always seems scrappier and it is usually more difficult to work out just what is going on. Ju-jitsu, by comparison, is clear-cut and precise, with attackers and defenders much easier to identify and no obvious winners or losers. Ju-jitsu is probably one of the most misrepresented and misunderstood martial arts being practised today. Even judoka and karateka who are quite knowledgeable in their own fields and in other related disciplines often have little or no understanding of what the practice and application of modern ju-jitsu entails.

Many judo players have an ingrained prejudice so far as ju-jitsu is concerned, believing it to be inferior to judo in every aspect, although many of those who believe this have never actually tried ju-jitsu. They tend to believe that judo develops a stronger, fitter body than ju-jitsu, while almost dismissing the fact that it also provides the practitioner with a tried and tested self-defence system. That the practice of judo has numerous benefits is indisputable, but whether or not it is *superior* to ju-jitsu is quite another matter. Any statement aiming to declare the superiority of one system over another is usually nothing more than a highly subjective value-judgement, not a fact.

Ultimately – despite their undoubted similarities – they are different activities, just as badminton is different from tennis and protracted comparisons are something of a pointless exercise. There is even a school of thought that argues that judo is just one more form of ju-jitsu. In the final analysis, choosing a martial art or sport to practise is very much a matter of personal preference and as long as your motives and desire to improve are sincere the outward form of your training matters only a little. The founder of aikido, Morihei Ueshiba, expressed a similar view very succinctly when questioned by a student as to which was the best martial art, replying 'The mountain does not speak ill of the river because it is lowly nor does the river speak ill of the mountain because it does not move.'

With the inclusion of judo in the Olympics, modern training techniques for strength and conditioning (which incorporate the use of weights and running) have made it vital that anyone competing at international level in judo be 'superfit' and equally strong. By way of examples the 1987 World Heavyweight Judo Champion, Grigori Veritchev of the Soviet Union, routinely performed repetition dead lifts with six hundred pounds on the bar. Even smaller fighters have remarkable strength and power: Shozo Fuji of Japan, four times a world champion, used to do rope climbing in training, using only one hand to climb the rope! Enormous physical power is one of the hallmarks of top-class judo fighters; it is no longer a secret – all the top medal winners are power athletes who, without exception, include strength-training using weights as part of their preparation.

The nature of ju-jitsu techniques and training, as well as its very different orientation (towards self-defence, rather than sport) makes physical power a less crucial factor than in judo and consequently more appealing to those less well developed physically – who are among those most likely to feel the need to take up and study a martial art for self-protection.

In particular, women, children and older people feel more confident in learning self-defence techniques based on co-ordinated movements that do not require the user to develop the immense physical power needed by the competitive judoka and which can be seen to be effective even against a physically much stronger attacker. One of the greatest strengths of ju-jitsu is its unpredictability. A karate man is likely to punch or kick, a judo man to grab or throw, a boxer to punch and so on, but ju-jitsu exponents are trained to employ any means possible to defend themselves and are taught to combine the methods of all the above systems. Of course anyone versed in ju-jitsu and regularly practising competition judo or karate has the best of both worlds. The emphasis in ju-jitsu training is upon speed and efficiency of execution. Competition in one of the other martial arts can teach the effective use of power – what works and what does not – even more thoroughly. Some modern ju-jitsu practitioners do have groundwork competitions and the creation of the 'SPORTKO' form of karate competition which allows striking, throwing, locks and strangles has led to some groups setting up their own style of sporting ju-jitsu competition, although in the interests of participants' safety many basic techniques cannot be permitted. Even so, it is one of the closest approximations that a sport can make to all-out combat – without ceasing to be a sport.

Although the maxim 'maximum effect from minimum effort' is common to both judo and ju-jitsu the arguments about the merits of power as against technique are as old as the martial arts themselves. However, it is undeniable that the combination of power *and* technique is devastating. Ito Mataemon, the founder of the Tenjin Shin'yo *Ryu*, who was renowned for the effectiveness of his *atemi-waza* and the need for practical realism in ju-jitsu, had this to say on the subject, 'The use of power in ju-jitsu is greatly necessary. But it is only when such power is not used in excess that it stands the test of the principle of *ju*. Another aspect of the use of power must be borne in mind, too. From the early stages of a trainee's development in ju-jitsu he must always be careful to avoid reliance on physical strength, for such is an obstacle in the way of his progress towards the gaining of skill in technique. After the trainee has developed a creditable technique, however, then the use of power is acceptable, and in fact absolutely necessary to his effectiveness in dealing with an adversary.' This should probably have been the last word on the subject, but it is a theme that martial artists never seem to tire of debating whenever they meet. In practical terms the great advantage that modern ju-jitsu has as a system is that it gives equal weight to the practice of striking and grappling techniques. Some people feel more at home with the striking arts and others with grappling and related systems, but ju-jitsu is unusual in that it combines both types of techniques; indeed it could justly be termed 'all-in fighting'.

The great appeal of modern judo and karate lies in the sporting element, in the thrill of competition, but for practitioners of classical ju-jitsu the idea of competition is effectively impossible, simply because the techniques they employ are designed exclusively for self-defence – and with that end in view are calculated to injure and disable any would-be assailant. This contrasts sharply with the supremely ethical system of Ueshiba aikido, where harming an assailant is antipathetic to the aims of the discipline. The contrast that exists within so many apparently similar martial arts is perhaps best explained by clarifying the meanings of the terms *jutsu* and *do*.

Jutsu and Do

The late Don F. Draeger, in his excellent scholarly volumes *Classical Budo* and *Classical Bujutsu*, defined the differences between 'budo' and 'bu-jutsu' by describing the former as 'the classical art of self-perfection' and the latter as 'the classical art of self-protection'. This distinction is quite crucial to an understanding of why judo flourished where ju-jitsu had floundered and why now, with heightened public awareness of the prevalence of social violence, ju-jitsu is enjoying renewed popularity.

Classical ju-jitsu was a product of a violent era. Although the name was given to the system of (virtually) unarmed fighting in the Tokugawa Shogunate era (1600–1868) the term is really generic and the system itself was much older, in fact deriving from a battlefield system of combat with or without weapons, a last resort for the warrior who found himself completely or partially disarmed. Ju-jitsu encompassed the use of whatever weapons might be available, with the unarmed techniques being the warrior's final option. Consequently practical effectiveness was the criterion for the development of techniques, many of which can only be described as vicious and savage. This viciousness was a hallmark of classical ju-jitsu techniques and totally acceptable as an aspect of a truly martial system, that is to say one designed for warfare. These same qualities, however, served to alienate people from practising classical ju-jitsu techniques in the modern period, beginning perhaps in the late nineteenth century which was a much more civilised and peaceful time.

Fortunately for the martial arts Kano recognised this and went to great pains to present his new system of judo to the general public as a development of great cultural worth, useful both for self-defence and as an effective method of physical education based upon strong ethical tenets. Kano's strongly developed philosophies made his judo very attractive and appealing to his countrymen who were then, as now, preoccupied by the necessity for self-improvement. Perhaps today the majority of typical judoka are not so high-minded and idealistic as the original students of Kano's Kodokan which may largely be due to the emphasis placed on sporting competition to the exclusion of other factors. Most judoka see their sport as a good way of keeping fit which also doubles as a usable method of self-defence, although few would deny that judo practice improves one's self-control almost as a matter of course. Probably the biggest difference between modern judo and judo as it was conceived by Kano is the way in which *kata* as a form of training is virtually ignored as well as the *atemi-waza* which formed such an important part of the original system. Not surprisingly, the modern ju-jitsu clubs are beginning to fill a gap created by current trends in judo which are drawing it away from its roots in ju-jitsu and towards a pure sport form. Many people have for a long time been dissatisfied with this tendency and are turning to ju-jitsu, which they are finding more and more appealing as a martial art form.

THE ORIGINS OF JU-JITSU IN BRITAIN

Many of today's sports-mad judoka tend to forget that judo was for all intents and purposes introduced to the general public in England by way of ju-jitsu performances in the country's music halls. The music halls were the great centres of live entertainment and as well as singers, dancers and comedians well known sporting personalities frequently appeared, including boxers and wrestlers, some of them world champions of the day. It was an Englishman, William Barton-Wright, who brought ju-jitsu to the United Kingdom, arranging demonstrations and challenge matches in music halls up and down the country. A civil engineer by profession but independently wealthy, Barton-Wright had studied ju-jitsu with Jigoro Kano in Japan and on his return to England founded his own self-defence system, naming it Bartitsu.

In an effort to publicise his system he imported in 1899, two Japanese experts, the Tani brothers, with whom he toured the music halls challenging all-comers. One of the brothers quickly grew homesick and returned to Japan after only a few months. The other, Yukio Tani, remained and became both wealthy and famous. A small man, Tani performed with another Japanese, S.K. Uyenshi, touring the country and taking on all-comers, including boxers, wrestlers, streetfighters – and drunks. Few of their opponents were trained professional fighters, but the rewards offered for beating either of the pair were high. Anyone staying on their feet for fifteen minutes could earn £20, the equivalent of ten weeks' wages for the average working man. The key to the ju-jitsu men's success was that they insisted that all their opponents dress in the unfamiliar jacket and belt, which gave them the advantage they needed, especially when they came up against skilful wrestlers. Tani's most difficult bout was against a wrestler, James Mellor, reputedly the World Lightweight 'Catch-as-catch-can' Champion whom he had to fight, because of a promoter's boast, without wearing the jackets. Tani won by two falls to one after a bout lasting an hour, giving some indication of his level of ability, although he often said there were many better than himself in Japan.

Indeed this proved to be true and Tani was eventually discredited in 1905 when he was comprehensively outclassed by another ju-jitsu expert, Taro Miyake, who was the 1904 All-Japan Champion. Tani had by now separated from Barton-Wright and had a new manager in William Bankier, but Tani's ex-manager, eager to discredit him and establish a new expert, had arranged for Miyake to come over from Japan. The younger, fitter Miyake was in top form and brushed aside Tani's challenge with consummate ease, destroying the myth of his invincibility which had made him so popular for so long. Ultimately no-one benefited from this since destroying the myth of Tani's invincibility also more or less ended ju-jitsu's music-hall appeal. Various nomadic ju-jitsu men sporadically turned up from Japan to make the rounds, but none achieved the fame, notoriety, and indeed wealth, enjoyed by Tani in his heyday. However, ju-jitsu clubs sprang up as a result of all the publicity and self-defence courses for ladies abounded.

The very next year saw the arrival in Britain of one of the key figures in the history of British judo, Gunji Koizumi, who was to found what is now the oldest judo club in Europe, the Budokwai, which opened in London in 1918 as the Budokwai ju-jitsu school.

What, then, is the history of the modern resurgence of interest in ju-jitsu? Perhaps one reason for the increase in interest in the more lethal and violent techniques of ju-jitsu, which have been put aside by practitioners and teachers of judo for some years, is the increasing prevalence in the media of incidences of violent crime. A heightened awareness of the need for a highly effective method of self-defence in an increasingly violent society has created a resurgence of interest in those techniques considered by the judo movement as too dangerous to use either in competition or in practice. At the same time the modern ju-jitsu movement has learned from judo and the ancient art is now presented in much the same way as judo once was; as a mental and physical discipline with a ready application to daily life. It is also presented as a healthy, sociable activity promoting self-confidence and physical fitness. Also the absence of any competitive element undoubtedly results in a lower injury rate than occurs in judo and karate.

The emphasis on performing techniques is also different. Many modern ju-jitsu teachers come into ju-jitsu through dissatisfaction with other systems of training, often blending, to good effect, knowledge gained through practising judo and karate in an eclectic way. While modern ju-jitsu training is a quite different activity to what was taught in the classical *ryu*, it retains much of value to members of a modern society. Good ju-jitsu dojo flourish in an atmosphere of co-operation; the real competition is with oneself. Students learn to defend themselves through the practice of armed and unarmed techniques of attack and defence but, equally importantly, they are taught respect for others. Courtesy, politeness and correct behaviour are stressed in all good dojo and the meaning of training is to endeavour to improve oneself as a person, not just as an athlete. The benefits of ju-jitsu training are consequently mental as well as physical; confidence will therefore increase along with co-ordination.

Whatever the different fruits, it remains to say that ju-jitsu is essentially the root-stock of modern Japanese martial arts and although the branches may be growing away from one another it seems certain that they have survived the test of time and will continue to flourish.

2   Philosophy and Ethics

BACKGROUND

One of the main reasons for the decline of ju-jitsu in nineteenth and early twentieth century Japan was the lack of any moral or ethical basis that justified its continued existence in a civilised society. Japan remains one of the most civilised places in the world with an incredibly low crime-rate by western standards, despite being one of the most densely populated countries on earth. In the late nineteenth century there was very little in ju-jitsu to commend or attract it to the average citizen. Ju-jitsu experts often belonged to the low life and used their knowledge to earn a living as anything from the equivalent of night club bouncers to yakuza bodyguards. The art had a bad reputation and was as highly regarded as the antics of modern day self-styled streetfighters.

Ju-jitsu was probably only saved from oblivion by the efforts of Jigoro Kano, the founder of judo, who paradoxically more or less displaced it in Japanese culture with judo. His Kodokan and the manner in which he transformed the art from *jutsu* (simple hand-to-hand combat) to *do* (spiritual way) ensured the survival of many of the teachings of the ancient schools. The famous victory of the Kodokan over the Yoshin *Ryu* ju-jitsu men had been in a large part a consequence of the development of the *randori* method of training. In a sense Kano had rediscovered how to apply the principle of *sen* (first strike) and still more subtle *sen no sen* (pre-emptive counter-attack or, as a

Fig 4   A winding throw.

western boxer might put it, beating the opponent to the punch) in training. The *kata*-form training of ju-jitsu had weakened the strategic application of the techniques so that the ju-jitsu exponent was essentialy passive until attacked, whereupon a counter-attack *(gon no sen)* would be permitted. Judo offered something new which was, in fact, the rediscovery of something old.

In essence judo can be considered as a maturation of ju-jitsu into a *do* form. The modern-day Olympic sport has moved a long way from its beginnings, too far for many conservatives who feel it has been trivialised by a one-sided sporting development. As a means of training, judo was originally intended to produce a well developed physique and character and to assist its practitioners with the socialisation process. Kano's judo was based on two important principles: *seiryoku zenyo* (best use of energy) and *jita kyoei* (mutual welfare and benefit). It was conceived very much as a vehicle for physical and spiritual education and its aims were no less than to perfect the individual. There were three aspects of training which comprised Kano's judo: *rentai-ho* (physical development, a strong healthy body), *shobu-ho* (skill in contest, requiring physical ability and mental determination) and, most importantly, *shushin-ho* (mental cultivation in a moral sense for the benefit of society as a whole, not just the individual). Kano actually felt that judo could contribute both to international understanding and co-operation and world peace.

The relevance of all these precepts to ju-jitsu is that the modern ju-jitsu teacher promotes very much the same ambience in the dojos as was encouraged in the original Kodokan, but neglects *shobu-ho* for the reasons already stated, concentrating on *rentai-ho* and *shushin-ho*, something which is not true of many modern judo clubs, where the emphasis is clearly on *rentai-ho* and *shobu-ho*. Without an ethical basis and a strong, clear philosophy any martial art becomes nothing more than physical training with a bag of, more or less, gymnastic, fighting tricks. Without a morally-based philosophy they do not evolve or develop and in many cases may not even survive.

A similar achievement to that of Doctor Kano, although perhaps of slightly lesser magnitude, can be attributed to the founder of aikido, Morihei Ueshiba. Ueshiba *sensei's* aikido is unique among martial arts in that it aspires to offer a non-violent method of self-defence which, in accordance with the Buddhist idea of *karma*, adds to the development of universal peace and love, rather than spreading further aggression and violence. Ueshiba aikido is founded on the highest principles of the martial arts and the master himself was attributed by his students with superhuman powers. As yet, none of his disciples has attained a level of ability or mastery comparable to that attributed to the master who died in 1969 at the age of 87.

Another factor worth considering is that had it not been for the growth of karate as a martial art many of the striking techniques of ju-jitsu would be less effective than they are. The *atemi-waza* of the classical *ryu* might otherwise have been lost to us. Aikido originally contained a great number of *atemi-waza*, but the change in emphasis that came about with the transformation of the activity into a quasi-religious route to the perfection of the character led to them being practised less and less.

The role of the ju-jitsu instructor is one which carries considerable responsibility and there is a school of thought which maintains that it is not enough to be a mere instructor showing students tricks, but that every dojo should have a real teacher or *sensei*. In the classical *ryu*, which were usually situated in rural peasant societies, the *sensei* effectively became a father to his students, not just teaching technique but a whole attitude to life, an entire philosophy. The same was true for many traditional karate dojo and arrangements existed where the students, in return for lessons and in some cases food, cleaned, cooked and otherwise worked in the school to pay their keep. In a traditional *ryu*, students were subjected to extreme hardship in order to develop character and spirit along with technique and, eventually, realisation. This process, which is extremely demanding and difficult to endure, progresses through the *gyo* stage (basic training) to the stage known as *shugyo*, or austere, unabated training, which in turn leads the student to the level of *jutsu* (technical mastery) and finally *do* (spiritual attainment). At the *shugyo* stage, catching and eating rats, in order to supplement the meagre diet with some animal protein, was not unknown among impoverished students of the martial arts, even as recently as twenty years ago. With the immense economic success that has taken place in Japan since the war, this kind of deprivation has virtually disappeared, although the training in Japan, especially in the university judo, kendo and karate dojos, remains extremely arduous.

The ethical attitudes embodied in the various martial arts differ from one another, but all have in common a moral basis. Karate has its variant styles, philosophies and attitudes, but the *shotokan*, founded by Gichin Funakoshi and one of the best established and most respected systems, is representative of the importance attributed to behaving correctly. Funakoshi himself wrote in his master text, *Karate-do* (*My Way of Life*), 'Karate begins and ends with courtesy'. Yamaguchi Gogen, the founder of the Goju *Ryu* style of karate, described his art as 'a way of peace' and maintained that it leads to a non-aggressive way of life; 'Karate *do* means not to be beaten, but also not to strike others.' Otsuka Hidenori, founder of the Wado *Ryu* (literally, the way of peace) blended the severity of the Okinawan karate styles with the principle of flexibility (*ju no ri*) that underlies ju-jitsu and saw karate as a spiritual way to achieve peace and harmony. The Wado *Ryu* syle was founded in 1939 and is one of the most suitable for study for ju-jitsu exponents, because of its essential compatibility with the principle of *ju*.

THE PRINCIPLE OF JU

The principle of *ju* is the central notion of ju-jitsu; it is an abstruse and abstract philosophical notion often misinterpreted. Pliability is perhaps the best translation although teachers often explain it as yielding. Another interpretation is adaptability, for the effective utilisation of the principle involves yielding and stiffening or resisting, not simply giving way. One of the major difficulties inherent in grasping this concept is the extent to which it has been interpreted throughout the centuries. The history of ju-jitsu is long and enmeshed in the development of the classical *bugei* or bu-jutsu (martial arts) and their subsequent transition into classical budo and ultimately the modern bu-jutsu and budo.

The techniques of classical ju-jitsu derived from *kumi-uchi*, or battlefield close-quarter combat, which in turn had developed out of sumo grappling and striking techniques dating from pre-Christian times. As *kumi-uchi* had been devised for dealing with armoured foes, the importance of striking techniques – relatively ineffective against an armoured man – was very limited and grappling methods for throwing the opponent to the ground where he could be choked, trampled or stabbed to death, took precedence. The Katori Shinto *Ryu* developed a system of grappling within its curriculum called *yawara-ge*, which was to influence pro-

21

foundly the development of ju-jitsu. A host of other *ryu* which had been created in response to an age of warfare and bloody violence all had their specialist techniques for defeating an enemy, whether armed or unarmed, but their essence was entirely combative in the military, not the sporting, sense of the word.

The term ju-jitsu was applied to a body of techniques which became popular for self-defence in a social context as distinct from the military, in the Edo period (1600–1868) when, under the rule of the Tokugawa Shogunate, Japan enjoyed a period of peace. Methods of unarmed fighting were evolved for dealing with routine social violence by the common people alongside the battlefield ju-jitsu of the classical *ryu*. The ju-jitsu of this period was popularly known as *yawara* among the common people who were prohibited from carrying weapons and its techniques were undoubtedly influenced by a Chinese-born naturalised Japanese man named Ch'en Yuan Pin.

Ch'en Yuan Pin, or Chin Gempin in the Japanese, (sometimes shortened to Chingen), taught techniques of *ch'uan fa* (fist way) which developed into Japanese kempo, which in turn were subsumed into the ju-jitsu systems taught in the seventeenth century. The use of striking techniques, effective against unarmoured opponents such as the average man in the street might encounter, became popular among the common people at this time.

A host of terms existed in the Edo period to describe systems similar to ju-jitsu, including *wajutsu, tai-jutsu, yawara, kogusoku, koshi-no-mawari, yawara-ge, torite*. All of these were battlefield systems incorporating hand-to-hand fighting with weapons, but alongside them bastardised versions were taught to the ordinary people for dealing with combat situations that arose in daily life, arrest techniques and self-defence for policemen and the like, leading to two quite distinct mainstream forms of ju-jitsu-type systems developing simultaneously. All of these systems operated by utilising the principle of *ju*; yielding when necessary, becoming pliant and supple in response to attack. This is apparent in the Edo forms into which they evolved; aikido and judo.

Serious students of ju-jitsu ought to learn as much as possible about their chosen art and other martial arts. They are in the same position with regard to their art as T. S. Eliot describes in *Tradition and the Individual Talent;* they confront the inherited cultural accretions of centuries and face the same task of inspection and selection as the famed poet and literary critic.

One of the major weaknesses of most martial arts is that they are essentially conservative activities which tend towards ossification. The hallmark of modern ju-jitsu, however, is its ability to assimilate change, whether it takes the shape of new, more scientific training methods or new strategies and techniques for dealing with new situations and weapons. It is a modern discipline designed to provide the practitioner with a system of exercise and self-defence. In a very important sense it is what its practitioners make it. The choice is yours.

If you are ever fortunate enough to see top Japanese martial arts experts watching their colleagues in action you will see that their attention is absolutely riveted to what takes place before them, because they are always alert to the opportunity to learn. The Japanese have an expression for learning by watching which roughly translates as 'stealing with the eyes'.

When looking for an instructor, it is most important to be selective. The good western instructor, while not a *sensei* in the Japanese sense of the word, should play a major part in inculcating correct attitudes and good character in his students. Visit as many dojos as possible, practise, observe and decide which has the highest standards and the approach which will, in the end, be the best for you. Ultimately, everyone is their own master and responsible for their own individual actions and consequences in, as well as out, of the dojo.

3 Anatomy

One of the most important principles of modern ju-jitsu is finding an opponent's weakest point, based on a knowledge of anatomy and the body's basic processes. The effectiveness of *atemi-waza*, or pressure-point gripping attacks on nerve centres, is multiplied considerably by selecting the correct target area. One of the first things a student of ju-jitsu learns is basic anatomy and the location of the body's vulnerable areas. Of course, many of these vital points are common know-ledge while others are better known in the combat sports. The eyes, throat, nose, solar plexus and testicles are particularly likely to be the target in a street assault. The lower regions of the body are more likely to be the target in a kicking attack, while the face is more readily vulnerable in a punching attack.

Atemi-waza, however, is a far more exact science than the crude blows of the typical streetfighter or mugger and there are far more target areas for a wider range of techniques than the untrained person could possibly guess. There are three main regions of the body from the point of view of applying striking tech-niques. These are: the head and neck; the trunk; and the lower limbs.

The head is, of course, the command centre of the body, housing the brain and most of the major sense organs, including the eyes, nose, ears and mouth, all of which are sensitive to pain and easily damaged. Blows to the head can easily render a person unconscious and if exces-sively powerful can cause brain damage

Fig 5 Using a wrist-lock and body-weight to control an assailant.

or even kill. Deaths in combat rarely occur from being struck with a single blow and tend to result from the cumulative effects of severe beatings, often coupled with extreme exhaustion, as in the case of pro-fessional boxers. The effectiveness of knock-out punches results from the impact of the fist causing the brain to move inside the skull. This causes the individual to black out. The point or side of the jaw are the areas most boxers aim

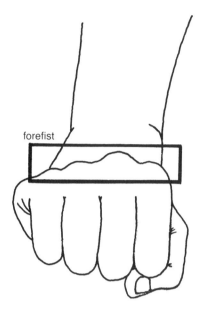

forefist

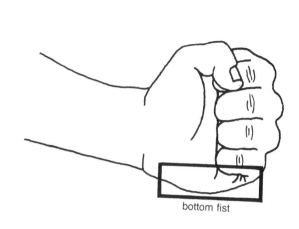

bottom fist

Fig 6–9 *Some of the weapons of the body used in* atemi-waza. *This (Fig 6) shows the fore-fist.*

Fig 7 *The bottom fist.*

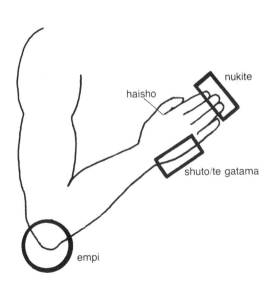

nukite

haisho

shuto/te gatama

empi

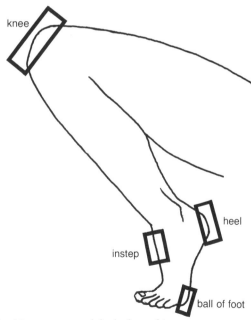

knee

heel

instep

ball of foot

Fig 8 Shuto *(knife hand)*, nukite *(extended fingers)*, empi *(elbow)*, haishu *(ridge hand)*.

Fig 9 *More weapons of the body used in* atemi-waza; *the knee, the instep, the ball of the foot and the heel.*

25

to hit since impacts here facilitate the shaking movement of the head that leads to the knock-out effect. Knock-outs occur occasionally in other sports, such as semi-contact karate when the odd accidental or uncontrolled blow lands – again usually to the jaw. Basically, every case of a knock-out blow causes concussion and minor brain damage, so experimenting by knocking out partners in training *cannot* be recommended.

The implications of the effectiveness of the punch to the jaw for ju-jitsu students concerned to develop their ability to protect themselves are obvious. In addition to being a very quick and effective method for incapacitating an attacker, it is also a target that is relatively easy to hit and one that is safe, from the point of view of applying ju-jitsu for self-defence. Moreover, it is safe in terms of the amount of damage that such a blow will inflict on an assailant; whilst a knock-out punch to the jaw does no one any good, an equally hard blow delivered to the temple or wind-pipe, for instance, could quite easily kill the person.

A blow to the eye or eyes by someone trained to hit can cause severe tearing of the skin as well as permanent eye damage, perhaps even partial or total blindness. The potential seriousness of attacking the eyes should not be underestimated; a complete loss of vision can result from eye damage incurred whilst fighting. Many boxers are forced to retire because the retina has become detached – caused by taking one punch too many – and many fights are stopped because of cuts on or near the eye since such cuts may constitute a great hazard to a fighter's health. Punching someone in the eye, especially without gloves, is an extremely vicious and danger-ous form of attack, only for use in dire emergencies. The knock-out blow to the jaw must be preferred every time. Class-ical *atemi-waza* to the eyes were designed for life-and-death struggles, where neither the well-being of the assailant, nor the legal consequences of any damage inflicted were of any concern to the person being attacked.

The eyes remain a very vulnerable target and can be effectively attacked in order to distract an assailant and apply a throw or a locking technique. However, it would be difficult to justify inflicting serious injury unless an attacker were armed. As the punishment should fit the crime, so the degree of force used should corres-pond to the seriousness of the threat an assailant offers. In the case of women, children or old people seriously threatened by an adult male attacker, aiming for the eyes may be the best chance for survival.

Blows to the nose are excruciatingly painful, invariably causing bleeding, impeding breathing and making the eyes water, so causing vision difficulties. The nose is particularly vulnerable to open-handed blows striking in an upward direc-tion. If the nose is broken, permanent disfigurement can result and breathing becomes impaired.

The mouth is similarly vulnerable and the lips are prone to splitting and bleeding if a punch lands on a mouth unprotected by a gum-shield. The gum-shield prevents the teeth from being knocked out and also from splitting the insides of the mouth. A punch in the mouth can also lead to injury to the hand if the fist comes into contact with the teeth.

Punching an attacker in the forehead or the back of the skull is likely to do as much damage to your own hand as to your assailant's head, perhaps even more. The head (as opposed to the face) is a particularly dangerous place to punch any-one and indeed one of the main reasons

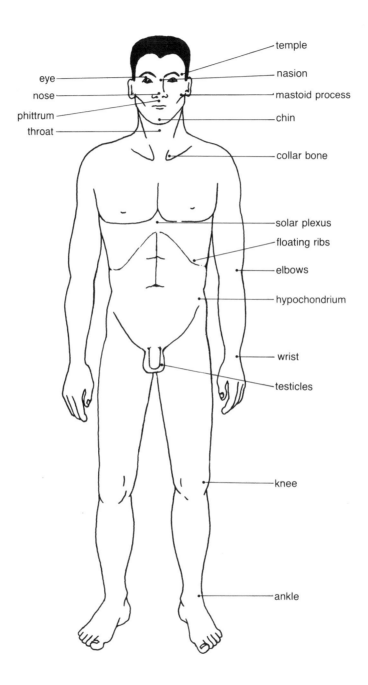

Fig 10   The main target areas (vulnerable points) of the body.

that boxers wear gloves is to protect their hands. The outlawed bare-knuckle style of fighting frequently saw hand injuries, caused by hard heads, deciding the outcome. Incidentally, it is highly unlikely that the old-time prize-fighters could punch as hard or were as fit as modern-day boxers. Improved training methods and hand protection in the form of bandages and gloves allow fighters to generate more power and punch harder than ever before. Obviously, when defending yourself against an attacker, there is never sufficient time to bandage up your hands and put gloves on, so it is imperative that ju-jitsu practitioners train to make a 'proper fist' in order to be able to hit effectively and not damage their hands in the process. The formation of a correct fist has always been a hallmark of Japanese karate systems and students have always trained, with some frequency, on the *makiwara* (a wooden post covered in straw) to forge their weapons.

Those martial artists who, for whatever reasons, prefer not to perform hand-conditioning drills (which have been much criticised) are advised to develop striking techniques targeted on the soft areas of an assailant's body. The solar plexus is just such an area, being a large nerve group located just below the point of the sternum or breastbone. It was made famous as a target area in the west long before the popularisation of ju-jitsu, when Bob Fitzsimmons became the Heavyweight Champion of the World by knocking out Gentleman Jim Corbett with a punch to the solar plexus. In the untrained person it remains a very vulnerable area, but combat sportsmen such as boxers, kick-boxers and full-contact taekwondo fighters perform lots of abdominal conditioning to build up and tone the muscle necessary to protect the area.

As well as those target areas on the face mentioned earlier, there are other places that cannot be protected by any amount of conditioning, in particular the throat, kidneys and testicles.

The throat can be attacked with striking techniques which cause a reflex gagging action as the person struck gasps for air. The knife hand, straight-finger jab and extended knuckle strike are best for attacking this area, as the windpipe is protected on either side by the sterno-mastoid muscles of the neck. The throat is often an awkward target since experienced fighters keep their chin tucked low, which tends to protect this area very effectively.

The kidneys are located in the back just below the ribs and when struck cause a particularly sickening pain akin to that caused by a blow to the testicles. Obviously the attacker must have his back turned, or at least be sideways-on, in order for a strike there to be feasible, but this position can easily be achieved once any sort of punching attack is made. When an attacker is on the ground, perhaps after being thrown, he will frequently attempt to protect the front of his body by curling up in a ball, but in so doing he exposes his kidneys to serious injury from stamping kicks, the knee-drop or punches.

The testicles are probably the weakest point on any man and are susceptible to striking, kicking and squeezing attacks. They are generally indicated as the best target for a woman threatened by rape. Low kicks or knee strikes are effective when standing, as indeed is the low punch. When fighting on the ground it can be difficult to generate sufficient force for an effective strike, but grabbing and squeezing is a distinct possibility.

All of these areas above are very sensitive to pain and a hard blow should incapacitate or badly injure most assailants.

Ju-jitsu techniques can also be directed against the joints of the body, the fingers, wrists, elbows, ankles, knees and neck. All joints are designed to move through certain ranges of movement which vary from individual to individual. Ju-jitsu *kansetsu-waza* employ the principle of forcing the joint through a range of movement for which it was not designed. This puts severe strain on muscles and especially on ligaments, which frequently tear when a joint is moved beyond the extremity of its normal range and so becomes dislocated. Many of the body's joint structures are interdependent and pressure applied on one can be transmitted through to another. The interrelation between elbow and shoulder is the most obvious case; frequently a technique designed to lock the elbow, such as *ude-garami* or *waki-gatame* will lock the shoulder also. This is often a result of the person being locked twisting to alleviate the pressure of the initial attack and so 'spreading the load' or simply a result of limited mobility.

The neck tends not to be thought of as such but it is indeed a vitally important joint. Despite being protected by strong muscle groups (at least in some cases) the neck is still extremely vulnerable to a variety of methods of attack. Neck locks, strangles and chokes can all be applied with sufficient force to kill. Striking techniques, however, would generally need to be extremely powerful in order to be lethal. Any attack to the neck, particularly locking techniques, can have a paralysing effect because of the neck's connection to the spine and central nervous system. Strangles and chokes can be most usefully employed as they can be used to render an assailant unconscious before releasing him, so removing the need for any further injury.

Although both are described as *shime-waza* there is an important distinction between a choking attack and a strangle that should be clear in the student's mind before using such techniques. A strangle such as *nami-juji-jime* works on the principle of cutting off the blood supply to the brain by applying pressure against the carotid artery in the side of the neck. Cutting off the blood supply to the brain deprives it of oxygen and so causes unconsciousness; it is normally quite painless.

In contrast, a choke is effected by applying pressure with the bony inside edge of the wrist against the windpipe or trachea and then squeezing, which has the effect of cutting off the air supply to the lungs. This, too, will cause unconsciousness, but is normally accompanied by frenzied resistance because of reflex panic and struggling brought about by the attendant choking or drowning sensation. Alternatively, unconsciousness can be almost instantaneous. Many *shime-waza* combine both choking and strangling effects to varying degrees. It should always be remembered that *shime-waza* can kill if applied with a jerking action or maintained after the assailant has been rendered unconscious. Chokes are distinctly more dangerous since there is a risk of unintentionally crushing the trachea which is likely to cause death.

The other joints of the body are more easily attacked by locking techniques than strikes, especially when fighting on the ground and techniques exist to sprain, dislocate and break. The knees, elbows, ankles and shoulders are all vulnerable to such techniques. The knee is also a particularly suitable target for kicking techniques and, despite being very strong in certain positions, if struck with a blow of only forty or so pounds of pressure, *laterally*, it will normally dislocate. Stamping kicks are usually employed for attacking the knee from the front or the side and have the advantage that they can be used at long range before an attacker gets close enough to land a punch or grab hold of his intended victim. The knee can also be stamped on from behind. If this method is chosen it will cause the leg to bend and assist in forcing an attacker to the floor.

Other target areas which can be hit to knock an assailant to the ground include the liver, spleen, floating ribs and the occipital (back of the head). The pit of the stomach (the area below the belt in boxing parlance) is not as well protected by muscles as the upper abdomen, and vital, vulnerable organs are located there.

It can therefore be effectively hit with kicks or punches. Just beneath the heart is a vulnerable spot and the armpit, although generally difficult to attack is a major nerve centre which can be exposed when making certain punching or stabbing attacks. Even the thigh contains vulnerable nerve centres as anyone who has ever been given a 'dead leg' will agree. The nerve centres of the thighs are in fact major target areas for kicking attacks in both Kyokushinkai karate and Muay Thai kickboxing and if trained to kick in the techniques of either of these fighting systems it is a surprisingly simple matter to 'drop' an untrained attacker with a leg kick.

4 Basics and Breakfalls

Ju-jitsu is practised in a dojo or training hall which contains a large *tatami*, or mat, on which students go through their paces; practising kicks, punches, blocks, throws, holds and locks. In a good dojo the techniques are performed quickly and crisply flowing from one into another. The co-operative nature of the training ensures that injuries are rare, but one of the most important elements for ensuring that injuries are minimised is learning the correct falling techniques.

Falling techniques are a vital part of ju-jitsu training; it is essential that all trainees know how to fall in order to facilitate throwing practice and to avoid training injuries. Training in *ukemi-waza* also improves confidence, co-ordination and agility – especially the latter, which is a vital component of effective combat skill. Falling techniques are also known as breakfalls – because you use them to break your fall.

Fig 11 *Breaking an assailant's balance.*

ETIQUETTE AND COURTESY

Etiquette and courtesy are intrinsic components of all genuine martial arts and there are a number of very strict rules that have to be observed by anyone practising ju-jitsu. First and foremost, no one on the mat should ever do anything with the intention of harming anyone else. Practitioners bow to one another before and after practising techniques. This indicates sincerity and mutual respect, qualities which help to develop confidence and trust in one another – important when potentially injurious techniques are being practised. Students and teachers should always wear a clean *gi*; this is simple personal hygiene and should not need to be stressed. Finger- and toe-nails should be kept short to prevent accidental cuts to others or even nails being ripped off by getting caught in the *gi*. Footwear should be worn walking to and from the *tatami*, again for reasons of hygiene. Bleeding of any kind should be treated urgently and any spilled blood immediately cleaned up. Students should, of course, not be allowed to continue training until all bleeding has stopped. The session should always begin with the entire class lining up and kneeling down to bow to the *sensei* (teacher) who returns the bow. The class should end in this way too. The instructor should normally be addressed as *sensei* in the dojo and on the mat must always be obeyed without any argument.

TAI-SABAKI (BODY MOVEMENT)

In most clubs, students learn about *tai-sabaki* or body movement before learning to fall. This involves studying and then practising a series of steps and body movements which are an indispensable part of ju-jitsu. *Tai-sabaki* can refer to anything from side-stepping a kick or ducking a punch, to blocking a throwing attack. As an example, a very basic *tai-sabaki* movement involves standing with your feet shoulder-width apart, in *shizentai* (natural posture). Pivot on the ball of your right foot and take your left hip through ninety degrees to your rear. Face forwards, turn your shoulders and hips in a smooth movement, so you are standing sideways-on, still facing in the original direction. This movement can be used to side-step kicks and punches.

THE JU-JITSU UNIFORM

The training uniform worn in ju-jitsu varies from association to association and indeed from club to club. Most ju-jitsu students train wearing the white cotton *gi* used for karate, or the heavier double-weave judo jacket type. In some clubs the black belts may wear the black *hakama* (split skirt) worn by aikido dan grades; this may be considered traditional dress. With the 'westernisation' of ju-jitsu, however, there have been some interesting departures from the traditional ideas of correct dress; blue, yellow and red *gi* are not unknown, particularly in the USA. The World Ju-jitsu Federation insists that its members wear a white karate style uniform with a stripe down the sides. Badges are also worn as an indication of rank or grade in conjunction with the normal array of coloured belts that characterise the rank systems of the Japanese martial arts. The real importance of the uniform is that it should allow unrestricted movement, stand up to the wear and tear of training and be kept clean.

BREAKFALLS

The Front Breakfall

The front breakfall or front-line down technique (not to be confused with the forward breakfall in which you roll) involves diving face down on the ground and catching yourself on your hands, ending in a position similar to a press-up. This fall prevents injury when thrown with a double-ankle grab pick-up from the rear. It can also be useful in any situation where you trip forwards and rolling is impossible. Basically, you reach for the ground at speed before you impact, and use your palms and perhaps forearms as though they were shock absorbers, allowing your head and body time to decelerate. The most important aspect of this fall is that it ensures your face does not smash into the ground; it also helps to avoid injury to the abdomen and knees. As with all breakfalls, you should ensure that your mouth is closed and your tongue is not sticking out.

Forward Rolling

It is not always a good idea to breakfall to the front in the face down position; indeed it is often preferable to roll, with a particular technique, and then come to your feet afterwards.

The major difference between the forward breakfall in judo and ju-jitsu is the way ju-jitsu exponents come to their feet facing in the direction from which they have just fallen. It is standard practice to roll and come to your feet, simultaneously turning to face your opponent in a defensive guard. Judoka, on the other hand, roll, stand up and usually carry on walking.

The forward-rolling breakfall is easier to perform the faster the trainee is moving; a jog is probably the best rate of approach for practising the technique. It can be performed to the right or the left, so that you are able to take a throw made left- or right-handed. If you are thrown with right *ippon-seoi-nage* the right side of your body is controlled by your opponent and you go over the right shoulder of the thrower who pulls through on your right arm to spin you on to your back, with your left arm striking out at the mat just before your back hits the ground. This breaks your fall and avoids the possibility of damaging your arm by the weight of your body falling on top of it. Try to keep as relaxed as possible and exhale as you hit the mat to avoid being winded by the fall. It is also possible to use the legs to break your fall by striking the ground with your heels before your back hits the mat.

The forward-rolling breakfall is often used as a warm-up technique with trainees in effect throwing themselves while going through gymnastic routines including falls, cart-wheels and handsprings. When you perform the forward-rolling breakfall you should aim to simulate the effect of being thrown and so should lean into the fall with the side of your body. It may help if you think of placing your hand on the floor and then diving over it. Keep in mind that your head should be kept tucked in and should at no point touch the ground; that the leading hand should be held shoulder-high with the arm fully extended away from your body and with the palm down, reaching out all the time with your hands.

The recovery from the rolling breakfall is important in ju-jitsu training. Practise using the momentum of the roll to bring you to your feet and immediately turn to face the direction you have just come from. Some schools advocate keeping both legs bent and then using the straightening action of the legs to come to your feet while others prefer to bend one leg underneath the other to spring up and so allow a quicker turn to face an attacker who may be moving in to follow up a throw with kicks and punches. Always remember to keep your guard up as you come to your feet and turn.

Side Breakfalls

Initially the side breakfall is often taught with the student in a squatting position. To practise the technique you simply extend one leg in front of you and topple to the side, striking the mat with the palm of your hand as your hips touch the ground. Exhale on impact to ensure that you are not winded by the fall. Some schools teach their students to *kiai*, to yell forcefully to expel any air from the lungs.

Once the squatting version of the technique is mastered you should progress to doing the standing version. This can be done unassisted by swinging one leg in front and to the side, as if being thrown by a footsweep, and then toppling to the mat. In practice the side breakfall is necessary for receiving footsweeps such as *de-ashi-harai* and *okuri-ashi-harai* and some versions of *tomoe-nage*.

The Rear or Back Breakfall

The rear breakfall is important training for receiving throws to the rear which tend to produce very heavy falls. *O-soto-gari* and *ko-soto-gari* can give you a considerable shock if you have not been trained to fall correctly. The most import-ant point to stress is that you should keep your chin tucked in and avoid letting your head bang against the mat, which can cause concussion and even a neck injury if there is a whiplash effect from a particularly fast throw. When practising the fall unassisted, both your arms slam back against the mat at an angle of forty-five degrees to the body and your chin is kept tucked in so that the back of the head does not touch the mat. Slap the mat with the palms of your hands and be sure to exhale when you fall.

The Handstand Breakfall

The handstand breakfall is a useful agility drill that can help when being thrown by any technique which turns you completely upside-down, like *tomoe-nage* or *seoi-nage*. Unassisted, perform a handstand and then pull away your hands; as you fall on to your back slap the mat at an angle of forty-five degrees to your body with both hands.

The Somersault Breakfall

The somersault breakfall is exactly what its name suggests. Perform a somersault in mid-air, but instead of landing on your feet, as in gymnastics, hit the ground with your forearms in order to absorb the weight of your falling body and take the rest of the shock by landing with your feet on the floor. It is important not to let your hips or lower back hit the floor as these areas are not designed to handle such impacts. Somersault breakfalls may be necessary against types of *tomoe-nage*, wrist-lock throws and techniques where you are thrown over your partner's head.

5 Blocking Techniques and the Psychology of Ju-jitsu

By what I did yesterday, I win today.
That is the virtue of practice.
Song of the Hozoin school of Naginata-do, *c* AD 1600

Being able to block effectively an aggressor's attacks is at the heart of any defensive system and ju-jitsu is no exception. Ju-jitsu students practise blocking and evasion techniques against every conceivable type of attack from punches, kicks and grabs, to knife, club and gun attacks. While the beginner may be more concerned with developing fast, powerful kicks, punches and throws, without the ability to block, very little can be achieved. Pre-arranged sparring, in which one partner announces the intended technique and target area and the other blocks and counter-attacks, is one of the most important methods for building up good technique, as well as speed and, most importantly, correct timing and anticipation. The two prime components of ju-jitsu blocking technique are *tai-sabaki* (body movement, twisting out of the way or evading an attack) and *te-sabaki* (using the arm or hand to block or hold an opponent's limb). These elements must be combined effectively with an understanding of *ma-ai* (the evaluation of distance in a combat context) in order to prevent an attacker's blows from hitting their target. More important, however, than any of these technical considerations is the attainment of a state of mental readiness: if the mind is not right you cannot begin to fight.

THE MIND IN JU-JITSU

In the Japanese martial arts the training of the mind has always been at least as important as the training of the body – if not more so – and a variety of techniques and methods exist for psychologically conditioning the ju-jitsu trainee. Many modern schools ignore these aspects of ju-jitsu, which is a great pity, because they considerably enhance a person's ability to understand and implement what has been learned.

Meditation is perhaps the best known direct psychological training and its benefits are widely appreciated; many people who have nothing to do with martial arts also use meditation. The posture adopted for the traditional method of practising meditation is known as *zazen*. There are many different drills through which students are led until they are capable of meditating on their own. One classical drill involves sitting in *zazen* and imagining yourself on a mountain top. In front of you there is a white handkerchief covered by pebbles. The *sensei* tells you to empty your mind of everything and every time a thought drifts into your consciousness you should pick up a pebble and throw it away, the thought going with it. This is good training for stilling the mind. Such training greatly improves the ability both to concentrate and to identify needs and objectives more clearly.

Other drills involve imagining and relishing the things which give you greatest pleasure and then letting them go, discarding them. Conjuring up those objects that you most fear and then confronting them is also taught. The *sensei* will often tell students to imagine their worst fear and then growl at it, from the *saika tanden*, low in the stomach. The novice may find such practices artificial and embarrassing, perhaps even ridiculous, but nothing could be further from the truth. These are all exercises derived from the Zen Buddhist tradition intended to free the person from material considerations and emotional or worldly attachments, thereby allowing them uninhibited freedom to act.

Such meditational practices carried to the most extreme degrees were at the heart of the *samurai* warriors' resolute acceptance of death and the code of *bushido*, the way of the warrior. In *Ha Gakure, Hidden Leaves*, a book written by Yamamoto Tsunenori and other traditional *samurai* lamenting the passing of the old ways of *bushido* in the seventeenth century, the warrior philosophy is expressed most succinctly:

The way of the warrior is death. This means choosing death whenever there is a choice between life and death. It means nothing more than this. It means to see things through, being resolved. Sayings like 'To die with your intention unrealised is to die uselessly' and so on are from the weak Kyoto, Osaka Bushido. They are unresolved as to whether to keep to their original plan when faced with a choice between life and death. Every man wants to live. They theorise with staying alive kept in mind. 'The man who lives on having failed in his intention is a coward' is a heartless definition. That to die having failed is to die uselessly is a mad point of view. This is not a shameful thing, it is the most important thing in the way of the warrior. If you keep your spirit correct from morning to night, accustomed to the idea of death and resolved on death and consider yourself as a dead body, thus becoming one with the Way of the warrior, you can pass through life with no possibility of failure and perform your office properly.

This was the essence of the *samurai* ethos and an integral, indispensable part of the warrior's training for battle. For the modern day student of ju-jitsu, who is unlikely to be a soldier it may seem less relevant, but it can help considerably in the winning of the little battles that make up daily life. Meditation helps composure and self-control and alleviates stress; it can provide a route to the acceptance of death; it also enhances life. One of the reasons for practising mental control is that an uncluttered mind will quicken your reaction time. When blocking any attack the most salient factor tends to be the speed with which you recognise and respond to the initial attack. At a basic level of competence, reaction to attack is simply a conditioned reflex, but in the higher echelons of the martial arts this is not as desirable as it may seem. The beginner may think that being able to react 'without even thinking' shows the highest level of attainment, however, this is not always advantageous.

If people are trained to react reflexively in a certain way this can very easily be turned to their disadvantage. An obvious example of this in judo is a throw known as the twitch. Basically it is a technique which exploits a trained reaction. An untrained person attacked with a forward throw such as *harai-goshi* will generally be thrown without any idea of what happened to him. The trained individual, however, will know the correct blocking procedure; bending the knees, pulling back with the arm and thrusting the hips forward. This knowledge of defence can be exploited by the attacker, who feints the initial attack in order to get the thrusting reaction with the hips and then switches to a rear throw, in this case *ko-soto-gari*, to hook the person's legs away and upend his opponent in the direction in which the defender is applying force. Such techniques are doubly devastating – they combine forces of both attacker and defender.

A more sinister example of a similar phenomenon can be found in the annals of ju-jitsu. One of the major ju-jitsu schools in Tokugawa times had three of its top experts killed in a single week. All three men were killed at night, each by a single lethal blow, a knife thrust to the abdomen. Feuds among ju-jitsu schools were not uncommon and members of a rival school were suspected. It was inconceivable that three such highly trained individuals could be killed so easily by a single thrust, a thrust considered relatively easy to block at that, but the absence of any other wounds was irrefutable evidence that such was the case.

After much deliberation the school's remaining experts realised how it had been done. In those times there were two basic ways of using a knife to stab; an abdominal thrust or a down-swinging attack to the chest area. The expert could easily anticipate which of these two attacks was coming by the way the attacker held the knife. In a right-handed attack the knife would be held in the right hand and the left used to grip the scabbard as it was drawn. If the attacker intended to thrust to the abdomen he would reach to draw the knife from the scabbard with the palm turned down and thumb touching the hilt. If he intended to raise the knife up and stab down at the chest he had to grip the knife with his palm up and the thumb at the top of the handle.

Consequently, it was the position of the hand gripping the knife which betrayed the attacker's intentions. The rival school had realised this but had discovered a very clever ploy to get around the problem. The knifeman was taught to hold the knife reversed, with the handle in his left hand. This meant that when he raised his arm overhead in the dark the defender, having already noted the hand position, would use two hands in an X-block to stop the apparent downward attack with the right hand. In fact the right hand was only holding the scabbard and the knife, held in the left hand, could easily be plunged into the unguarded abdomen.

The important lessons from this story are not to fix your mind on things, as they are not always as they seem, and that skill in self-defence is not gained by slavish mechanical repetition. Technique has its place, but so too does instinct. The true expert must always be ready to adapt at a fraction of a second's notice.

A number of terms exist describing the states of mind to which students of the martial arts aspire and which are considered to be useful and desirable for progress.

Fig 12 Mu-shin; *the* kanji *for empty mind, a state of calm, relaxed alertness and of readiness for action.*

Mu-shin

Mu-shin, or empty mind, is a mental state in which students try to cut off thought and free themselves from distractions. This stopping of the thought processes, when successful, leads to a clear mind uncluttered by irrelevant or distracting ideas. The essence of *mu-shin* is in being ready and able to react without reflection in an emergency. It is essential not to be too tense since this can inhibit movement, nor so relaxed that you become careless, dreamy or sloppy.

Isshin and Zanshin

Isshin (one heart or mind) and *zanshin* (remaining heart or mind) are mental states or attitudes apposite to certain circumstances. *Isshin* is the spirit of abandonment, of throwing yourself into whatever you are doing with no thought for success or failure. In the case of judo or karate in free practice (*randori* or *kumite*) or contest (*shiai*) this means attacking with all your spirit, fearless of any counter-technique. If the attack is good you will succeed with your intention, if not, its intensity may at least unsettle your opponent. Attacking with this spirit in training – which is rather like risking everything on a single throw of the dice – will eventually bring results. *Zanshin* means retaining conscious (or unconscious) awareness in the course of an action, not exactly holding back, yet being aware of possible subsequent consequences to the initial attack. It is a wider, more enduring spirit than that of *isshin* which is focused like a laser beam and discharged. *Zanshin* is the consciousness both preceding and continuing after the attack. Another type of spirit in ju-jitsu is *fundoshin*, or 'immovable mind', and is a state of unshakable determination and is developed through training.

Different teachers prefer to cultivate different attitudes, according to what they feel needs emphasising in a particular individual. The important thing from a practical point of view is that trainees should be able to react spontaneously in an emergency without becoming confused or 'freezing'. They should understand that they can cope with differing situations in a number of different manners.

Perhaps the major problem, psychologically speaking, for many ju-jitsu exponents (and indeed other marital artists) at intermediate levels of ability is knowing how to assess and react to threatening situations; knowing when to attack and when to talk, when to wait and see and when to hit first. This is dealt with in detail in Chapter 6.

Ma-ai

Ma-ai (distance evaluation) is the area of ju-jitsu that deals with the use of the space between you and your attacker. It involves knowing when and where attackers come into range both from the point of view of their launching an attack and your being able to deal with it effectively. *Ma-ai* is the study of range (as used in the military context) applied to close-quarter situations. Obviously a man armed with a long stick becomes dangerous at a greater distance than a man with a club. Generally a person needs to be closer to punch than to kick and closest of all to launch a grappling attack. At six feet attackers may take a big step and launch a kick, at two they may just thrust at your lower abdomen with a knee. It is important to remember that being very close does not preclude many types of attack such as headbutts, upper-cuts, strangles and so

Fig 13   *The* kanji *for* isshin; *the one heart or one mind, the spirit of the all-out, decisive attack.*

on. Many of the old ju-jitsu and kendo schools trained to crucially precise distances, determined by the standardised nature of weapons. One school enjoyed enhanced success for a number of years by using swords a few inches longer than normal, which drastically threw out their opponents' long-established calculations, before their ploy was discovered.

In modern day ju-jitsu training it is most important to practise with as great a variety of partners of different heights as possible in order to grasp thoroughly the fundamentals of *ma-ai*.

BLOCKING

Covering Up

This is not actually part of blocking, but is worth mentioning at this stage as something to avoid. A bad habit many martial artists pick up from watching kickboxers and boxers is covering up. It certainly has a place in both those sports, but outside the ring there is no referee. You cannot afford to let yourself take punishment if attacked by a gang, for example. At such times the old adage that attack is the best form of defence is the best advice. It is also sensible to hit and run, if this is a possibility.

Obviously in a situation where you really cannot defend yourself it is better to cover particularly vulnerable parts as much as possible and to take any kicks or punches on the arms and legs rather than allow yourself to be hit in the body and head. However, it is a dangerous assumption that a group of assailants will stop kicking because they will feel you have had enough when you no longer represent a threat to them. People have died in such circumstances. Wherever possible, block and counter rather than covering up.

Techniques

The blocks in ju-jitsu differ from many hard styles of karate inasmuch as they employ the principle of *ju*, or pliability, rather than that of opposing force with force and smashing into the assailant's limb as the block is made, matching muscle with muscle, strength with strength. Blocks are made using twisting motions in order to deflect the force of an attack, so catching it and redirecting it. Some styles of karate, such as *wado ryu* and *shotokan* employ similar blocking techniques (which must be considered more scientific since they do not necessarily require the defender to have greater physical power and toughness).

There are some techniques in ju-jitsu which the beginner can easily mistake for blocks and which can break an attacker's arm as he punches or dislocate a knee as he kicks; these are called *ate-waza*. Blocks should be distinguished from *ate-waza*, however, for although the latter may function as blocks on occasion, they are actually striking techniques (such as the knife or ridge hand which are delivered to nerve centres in the opponent's arms or legs, or to the joint, as an attack is made). The double knife hand against a straight punch catching the elbow and wrist and pushing them in opposite directions to break the elbow is a good example of *ate-waza*.

Most blocks are performed using the open hand or the wrists and forearms, depending upon whether the technique is intended as a straightforward direct block, a deflection or a trapping block. Trapping blocks usually involve blocking with an open hand and then grabbing some part of the assailant's clothes or body, usually the sleeve or wrist. This grip can then augment a striking counter-attack or be

Fig 14–16   This sequence illustrates some simple principles of ju-jitsu attack and defence. In this illustration (Fig 14) the attacker (uke) is in left stance while the defender (tori) is in right stance.

Fig 15   Uke makes a stepping punch attack which tori avoids by moving back out of range and blocking with a knife-hand block.

Fig 16   Tori counter-attacks with a lunge punch to the jaw.

used to pull the attacker either off balance for a throw or into a locking technique.

There are generally considered to be four basic blocking movements: inwards, outwards, rising and downwards. These four blocks cover the whole body from the knees to the top of the head and should be sufficient for dealing with almost any unarmed striking attack. They are therefore an essential part of ju-jitsu.

With all blocks it is most important to get the power of your whole body into the technique. Although the hands, wrists or forearms may be the focus for the techniques, it is necessary to twist the upper body forcefully in order to get 'snap' into the block. As the blocking arm connects, the other hand should generally be pulled back on to the hip, karate-style, to magnify the power of the block. It is sometimes helpful to think of each block as a punch and snap it into place as fast as possible; such blocks are usually best followed up by striking techniques. At other times try being as loose as possible and stick to your opponent as you block, looking for the opportunity to pull him or her off balance and then throw. Both types of block have to be practised in the dojo, so that you can prepare for all eventualities.

The X-block is a two-handed block which is best employed against an armed attack. Its function is to stop, and in some cases trap your opponent's arm or leg preventing it from reaching its target in a situation where one arm would not have sufficient strength to do so or where the danger of the attack (perhaps a hand holding a knife) warrants it. Always bend your legs and forcefully straighten them

43

Fig 17   The basic downwards block against a punch to the body.

Fig 18   A palm-heel block, pushing the attacker's arm inwards to put him off
balance.

44

Fig 19   A trapping block . . .

Fig 20   . . . immediately followed by an elbow
strike.

Figs 21–5   This sequence illustrates basic blocking and countering. Here (Fig 21) uke attacks with a right-hand punch.

*Fig 22   Tori counters by stepping back on the right foot, moving to the left and using an **outer** block.*

Fig 23   Tori then follows up with a reverse punch.

Fig 24   Alternatively tori could have twisted the body to the right and used an inner block.

Fig 25   *Tori follows up by catching uke's arm with his right hand and
pulling him on to a left back-fist.*

Fig 26   *The X-block . . .*

Fig 27   *. . . immediately followed by a front kick.*

as you make a blocking action so that their strength, too, is transmitted into the action.

The feet, shins and knees can be used more effectively than the arms to block kicks because of the relatively greater strength of your legs, but cannot be used as quickly because hand–eye reaction time is biologically preconditioned to be faster. Stamping on an attacker's shin with the outside edge of your foot just as he attempts to launch a kick is a good example of applying *ate-waza* to block an attack.

6 Striking Techniques: Atemi-waza

If you feel that the teacher is a real teacher
Then give up your own ideas and learn
First verse of *The Hundred Verses of the Spear*

The striking techniques of ju-jitsu are many, varied and extremely effective. Their efficacy is further enhanced by targeting the most vulnerable areas of the body wherever possible. Such techniques, which rely upon impact to cause a concussive or incapacitating effect, are called *atemi-waza*.

These can be divided into two main groups; blows using the limbs of the upper body (including punches, chops and elbow strikes) and those using the lower limbs (kicks and kneeing attacks). What makes ju-jitsu so effective as a self-defence system is that these techniques can be combined with throws, sweeps, locks and strangles with a disconcerting suddenness almost impossible for the opponent to predict.

Originally in the early sixteenth century there was little to distinguish primitive ju-jitsu from indigenous sumo, or *kumi-uchi*, which was another form of combat devised for battlefield use. By the end of the Muromachi period (1600), however, there was a clear separation of the two, the earliest ju-jitsu school, the Takenouchi *Ryu*, having been founded in 1532. The early ju-jitsu schools were founded by the battle-hardened survivors of an age of interminable internecine warfare and

what was taught was called a martial art by virtue of the connection which existed with the code of *Bushido* which, with its strongly developed sense of aesthetics and spirituality, had a profound influence on the teaching.

The fighting system which was taught had developed out of battlefield survival techniques and was known by other names including *wa* (harmony) and *yawara* (hand-to-hand fighting). Striking techniques were taught, but given that in a battle the majority of *samurai* opponents were armoured, the kicks and punches were of limited value: armlocks, throws and strangles were considered to be more practicable against an armoured foe and so formed the basis of the system. Some 120 years later other names were given to what was being taught including *tai-jutsu* (body techniques) and *kempo* (a character read as kung fu in Chinese). Chinese boxing, or kempo, had arrived in Japan in 1645 in the person of a Chinese teacher, Chin-gen. This was at the beginning of the Edo period, the great age of peace during which there was no internal warfare and no battles were fought. Many of those practising ju-jitsu were *bushi*, warriors who were not *samurai* aristocrats and who were increasingly interested by

49

Fig 28   A knee strike.

Fig 29–36 One of the fundamental principles of ju-jitsu was that of using a striking technique to daze or distract an assailant and so facilitate the application of another technique. This sequence shows a defence against a lapel grab and punch attack. Initially (Fig 29) uke grabs tori's lapel.

Fig 30 Uke attempts a hooking punch which tori blocks.

Fig 31 Tori pushes down uke's punching hand and makes a quick back-fist strike to his face.

Fig 32 Tori immediately follows up with an ude-gatame straight armlock by driving his right arm down inside uke's left arm and then bending his arm to catch the back of uke's elbow with his right hand.

51

Fig 33 As tori completes the movement illustrated in Fig 32 he steps back, causing uke's arm to straighten. He then releases his grip on uke's right wrist with his left hand and consolidates the armlock, forcing uke forwards off balance.

Fig 34 Tori follows up with a hiza-geri, a knee strike to the face.

Fig 35 Tori then drives uke straight down on his face . . .

Fig 36 . . . and consolidates his position with a hammer-lock.

Fig 37 A jodan-mawashi-geri *(head-height roundhouse kick) from karate competition showing superb flexibility and control from the kicker. Note the foot of the supporting leg flat upon the floor, despite the height of the kick.*

striking techniques which could be successfully employed against unarmed attackers such as peasant robbers or belligerent drunks. Killing people in brawls was as illegal then as now, so mercenary swordsmen, *ronin* and the like needed less lethal techniques for dealing with life's little problems. Ju-jitsu expanded in this period, embracing the practice of all forms of weaponless fighting including the kind of punching and kicking techniques found in karate and kung fu. The techniques which grew in popularity in this era of ju-jitsu have more in common with those practised in the modern day, being intended for self-protection in unexpected social situations rather than a battlefield fight to the death.

STANCES

Many modern ju-jitsu clubs train using the popular modern karate-based stances as starting points for practising kicks and punches. However, in classical ju-jitsu, the emphasis was on fighting (in armour) with weapons and so grappling was the order of the day. Perhaps in order to allow the *bushi* sufficient advantage to stab their enemies with a short dagger, only two real stances, or more accurately postures, were employed. These were *shizentai*, or upright natural posture, and *jigotai*, or crouching defensive posture. For practising modern ju-jitsu, though, the basic forward and back stances and the 'horse' stance prove very useful, if not indispensable. This is because realistic punching and kicking attacks must be

53

made in order for students to learn to defend themselves effectively, as such attacks tend to be the most common forms of assault outside the dojo.

Actually to take up a stance in a self-defence situation would generally be both impractical and ostentatious. Stances are not secret weapons, but simply training aids designed to help develop leg strength and the ability to move fast. The theory is that the lower you make your stance and the longer your steps are, the better the training effect and ultimately the faster you become. There is nothing wrong with that. Unfortunately, the rules of sport karate tournaments insist, for very good reasons, that a technique must be generated from a recognisable stance in order to be considered powerful (effective). These have tended to create a false impression, or misapprehension, particularly in the minds of younger students and lower grades: you do not necessarily have to take up a stance in order to be effective in the street.

Consider the lethal punching power of world heavyweight boxing champion Mike Tyson. How often does he deem it necessary to take a stance before delivering a blow? The answer is, of course, that he never does so, and two of the reasons that he is so effective are his speed and mobility; these are not achieved by holding deep static poses in actual combat. This is not to say that he does not bend his knees before unleashing certain punches. Sometimes his fist seems to come from his heels! No criticism is implied of the use of deep stances in training as they are a tried and tested method of developing good basics, but in actual combat, such a stance is a body position that might only be adopted for a split second in order to execute a technique. There is nothing to be gained by attempting to scuttle around like a crab when defending yourself. Generally speaking, the faster a target is moving, the harder it is to hit.

TE-WAZA (HAND TECHNIQUES)

The Punch

Making a fist is the most basic – and one of the most important – aspects of correct striking technique. Open your hand as much as possible so that your palm is stretched. Bend your fist and second sets of knuckles until your fingertips are touching the fleshy pads at the base of your fingers on the inside of your palm. Close the fist gripping the index and middle finger with the thumb, which, beginners take note, must always be on the outside of the fingers, never inside. Almost all punches are delivered with the large knuckles of the index and middle fingers. Focusing the force into a small area makes the blow more effective.

The fist should be hard, tight, compact and able to withstand the impact of striking a bony part of an assailant's anatomy without fear of hand injury. Three points are necessary if this is to be achieved: correct formation of the fist; accuracy in delivering the blow; and hand conditioning. Hand conditioning and correct formation of the fist go together and can be achieved by a number of basic drills, including press-ups on the knuckles and the use of the *makiwara*, although many modern instructors regard *makiwara* training and the accompanying hand deformation it entails as unnecessary. Accuracy and correct delivery are best achieved by use of the focus mitts and punch-ball, power is developed on the heavy bag.

Many of the punches used in ju-jitsu are also found in most of the major sport karate schools. Ju-jitsu, however, makes greater use of circular punches for close-in fighting, such as hooks and upper-cuts, giving less emphasis in training to classic straight-line karate techniques such as the reverse punch, the back-fist and the stepping punch – even though such techniques score highly in karate competition. One of the reasons for this difference in emphasis is that the latter techniques have evolved very much as contest-winning movements under sport karate rules. In or out of the contest arena there is no disputing their effectiveness: straight-line punches are the fastest, but the rules of sport karate do not allow equally effective techniques, so far as pure self-defence is concerned, particularly as face contact with punches is not allowed. The other reason that hooks and upper-cuts are

appropriate to self-defence is that the body is generally much closer to the fist in such attacks, so making it easier to grab and then follow up with a throw.

A great moral dilemma that many law-abiding students of ju-jitsu must confront when they find themselves having to defend themselves for the first time is whether to strike the first blow or to wait until they are actually physically attacked. That attack is the best form of defence is an oft-quoted truism and its validity is difficult to deny. Some teachers maintain that you should never strike the first blow, others that the moral justification exists if you have reasonable grounds to believe that you are going to be assaulted.

The beauty of an *atemi-waza* technique such as an upper-cut or a short-range hook to the jaw is that they are difficult to predict, relatively low risk and instantly effective. If a would-be assailant gets hit

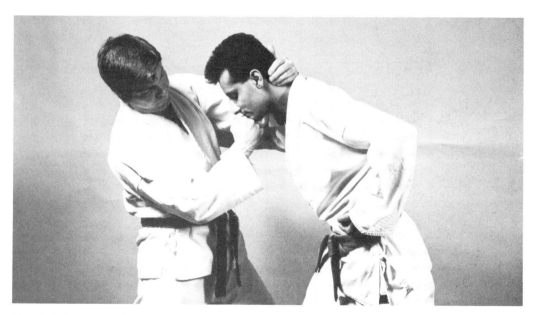

Fig 38 Pulling an attacker on to a punch to increase the effectiveness; it prevents the person being struck from 'riding' the blow since it does not allow movement in the direction of the blow.

with a knock-out blow before he sees the chance to attack, it is certainly effective as self-defence, but there is the danger that afterwards the law will regard such an incident as assault. The idea of the pre-emptive strike is entirely in keeping with classical ju-jitsu which was, after all, designed for warfare, but in a 'non-war context' it smacks to many people of deception and the sneak attack.

Some teachers advocate the pre-emptive strike as a method of preventing trouble-some situations and maintain that it is morally defensible to attack first if you are convinced that you are about to be the victim of an assault. Others more con-scious of ethics, but perhaps less pragmatic, insist that everyone be given the benefit of the doubt. Belligerent and abusive individ-uals do not always resort to physical violence and if ju-jitsu practitioners lose their nerve and precipitate violence them-selves then they are considered to have failed. Most people find their own ground somewhere between these two poles, giving the benefit of the doubt, wherever possible, to those who seem more irritating than dangerous.

Certainly where there is any threat of weapons being used or of more than one attacker it is entirely justifiable to go on the offensive if that seems to be the best strategy for dealing with the situation.

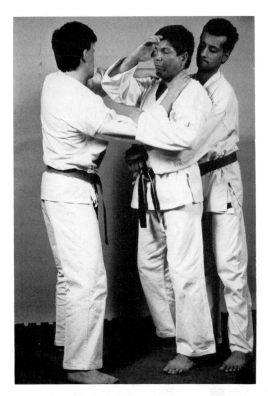

Fig 39–44 Atemi-waza *are indispensable against multiple assailants. Here (Fig 39) tori has been grabbed in a bear-hug, under the arms, from behind and is attacked from the front by a second assailant who tries to throttle him. Tori immediately counters with an elbow strike.*

Fig 40 *Tori follows this up with a reverse knife hand to the side of the neck and grabs his assailant's arm.*

Fig 41 *He knees his assailant in the groin, pulling him on to the blow.*

Fig 42 *Once the threat of being strangled is removed, tori immediately gives his other assailant a back elbow strike in the head.*

Fig 43 *If he fails to let go tori reaches down between his own legs and grabs his assailant's ankle.*

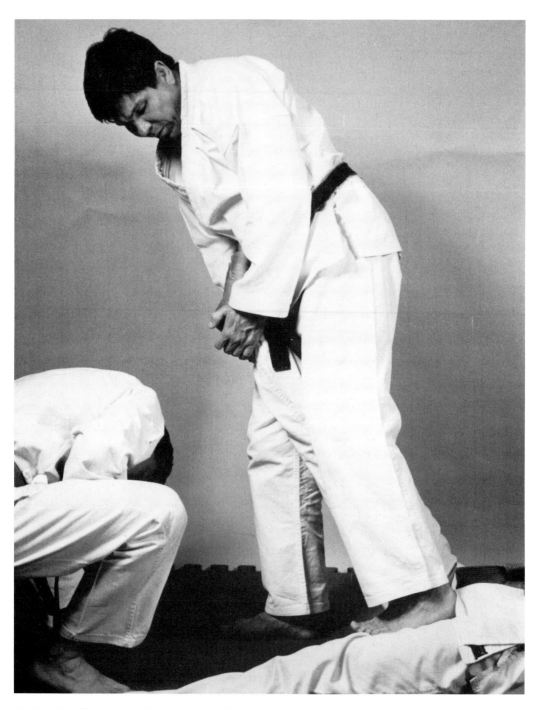

Fig 44   By pulling on the ankle and then straightening up, his assailant is thrown
to the ground, where tori finishes him off with a stamping kick.

These different strategies are known in Japanese as *sen* (first strike); *gonosen* (counter-attack); *sen-no-sen* (the pre-emptive strike). The latter is the most subtle and those without real experience of combat will find it difficult to grasp. It involves taking the initiative from an attacker at the first glimpse of his intention, knocking him out with an upper-cut as he pulls back his fist to hit you (for instance). It requires you to be completely in tune with your would-be assailant. You nip his attack in the bud rather than letting it happen and then countering. It is ethically superior to *sen* and safer than *gonosen*, but normally requires a high level of ability.

The Back Fist (Uraken)

This is, as the name suggests, a back-handed blow, but the energy of the *uraken* is focused in the same two knuckles of the hand as the 'fore-fist' or the reverse punch. It involves raising the fist to the opposite shoulder across the upper chest and snapping the hand out to the target with a rapid straightening of the arm. It is most effective as a kind of snapping punch, quickly fired and pulled back; moreover because it can be thrown to the front or side without changing stance, it is regarded as very versatile. Basically, it is either used vertically to attack the nose or horizontally against the side of the jaw, or, if the intention is more serious, to the temple (this is a potentially lethal blow). The back-fist is a minor weapon and the use of it does not generally expose the user to any great danger of being countered. Its ease of performance and speed make it a favourite opening gambit when self-defence is required.

The Reverse Punch (Gyaku-zuki)

This is the main weapon of many karateka. It is delivered as the attacker is approaching and can be used most effectively to the abdomen, chest or head. In a left-fighting stance, with your left hand and leg forward, the punch is performed by firing your right fist from the right hip, pulling the left hand back to cover your chest area, bending your front leg, straightening your back and twisting your hips. The standard forward stance, with the left leg and left arm forwards, is thus reversed, your leg staying forwards, but your right arm is extended and your left hand pulled back. The hand is normally held on the hip palm-up, rotating as it reaches its target to connect with the palm turned down. With the reverse punch, in particular, you should aim to punch right through the target.

The Snap Punch (Kazami-zuki)

Like the back-fist, the snap punch is essentially a minor technique. It is very fast without being a particularly heavy, knock-out type blow. It is normally used to attack the face as an 'opening-up technique' to stun or distract an attacker. It is a straight punch with the fist driven out directly from the shoulder, similar to a boxer's jab. It is delivered from the front hand by twisting at the waist and leaning in with the shoulder if you have your guard up, or from the hip if used as a shock tactic from a relaxed posture. It is equally easy to perform with either hand from a natural posture.

Stepping Punch (Oi-zuki)

The stepping punch involves taking a step and punching, so that as your right foot hits the ground in front of you your right fist arrives on target. This is a straight punch, much used as a standard form of attack when practising blocks and evasions. The striking area is the two large knuckles of the hand.

The Hook

A punch culled from the tradition of western boxing, the hook must be considered as one of the most effective punches in the book. It can be used as a long-range counter-punch, normally coming 'over the top' of a straight right. Frequently – because its trajectory makes it come in round the guard and strike the head from the side – it is difficult to see, and this is one of the reasons that boxers need good peripheral vision. It is just as useful when fighting at close range. Hooks to the body can cause severe damage, especially to the unconditioned non-athlete. The close-range hook to the head is a knock-out punch and you should train for this punch using the heavy bag as you would for body-shots. A good routine is to practise doubling up with either hand; alternating left to the body, left to the head, right to the body, right to the head. Bend your legs, straightening them as you land and twist from the waist and shoulders to get all your power into the hook. The full hooking movement is important; aim to punch through the target, turning the palm down as you land. The best target areas are the side of the jaw, just below the ribs and the kidneys. The striking area is not limited to two knuckles, as in *seiken* strikes, but rather the whole of the forefist.

The Upper-cut

This is another technique taken from boxing and is especially useful against people who keep their heads down or who hold a high guard to protect against hooks. Again it is a knock-out technique, normally targeted on the point or side of the jaw. The striking area can be the two large knuckles or the whole of the fist.

The Hammer-fist (Tettsui)

Sometimes called the bottom fist, this is a useful weapon; the fleshy edge of the palm is the normal striking area. It is most effective in finishing off an assailant who

Fig 45–7   *Sometimes ju-jitsu techniques are simplicity itself, but effective none the less – as in this defence against a wrist grab using* atemi-waza. *Here (Fig 45)* uke *grabs* tori's *wrist.*

Fig 46 Tori immediately counters with an upper-cut.

Fig 47 If necessary, tori follows the upper-cut with a rising elbow strike.

is on the ground when a punch might not be practical. Target areas include the collar-bone, testicles, the back and the bridge of the nose.

The Knife Hand (Shuto or Tegatana)

The knife hand is largely used for making blocks against punching attacks, but can also be delivered to the neck, throat and nose, with devastating results. The hand is held rigid with the fingers slightly curled and, as in the hammer-fist, the striking area is the fleshy edge of the hand. As well as being used in a downwards chopping motion it can be done reversed, like a back-fist. The knife hand is a favourite technique for demonstrations of breaking

prowess and is used for splitting boards, tiles and even bricks.

The Palm Heel Strike (Teisho)

This is an open-handed strike using the heel of the palm. It is often used for light, slapping, blocking techniques and can also be delivered as a downward strike or as a mid-way blow between an upper-cut and a straight punch. In the latter case it is frequently aimed at the base of the nose or the point of the jaw, both of which lift the head and render an attacker off balance to the rear, setting him up perfectly for a variety of rear throwing techniques, particularly *o-soto-gari* and *ko-soto-gari*. There is a variation known as *tanagokoro* which is basically a slapp-

61

ing attack derived from sumo. When both hands are used to clap an assailant's ears the effect is normally to rupture the eardrums; great care must obviously be taken when practising this technique.

The Spear Hand (Nukite)

This is also known as the straight-fingered jab. It looks like a knife hand, but the points of the fingertips are the striking area, rather than the edge of the hand. It is generally used for thrusting at soft target areas, such as the eyes and throat.

The Ridge Hand (Haishu)

This can be used to attack the ribs, face, or groin area. The striking area is the index-finger side of the hand. The thumb is kept bent and close to the palm, or straight with the index finger curled around the tip of the thumb.

The above are some of the major techniques focused through the hands – this is by no means an exhaustive list, but the hands are not the ju-jitsu exponent's only weapons; the elbows, too, can be used at close range to smash into an assailant and can inflict terrible damage very quickly. The elbow can be used against an assailant facing you, either as an upper-cut to the jaw or as a forearm smash-type hook to the face or head. Rear elbow strikes can be made by spinning into the attack, or when attacked from behind, either as body blows to the ribs (or solar plexus) or as knock-out attacks to the head. The elbow strike can also be used downwards by lifting the hand above the head and then dropping the body-weight into the blow. The striking area is usually the point of the elbow.

KICKING TECHNIQUES

Kicking techniques are an important element of ju-jitsu training. Generally speaking, the legs are up to four times stronger than the arms, they are, of course, also longer and, in daily life at least, protected by shoes.

Kicks can be used at low level for attacking the ankles, feet and shins, largely to distract an assailant by inflicting pain. They can be used to incapacitate by attacking the knee joint, the pit of the stomach or the testicles without any need for great flexibility. Above waist level, the midsection and ribs are natural target areas, but to kick effectively any higher requires good flexibility in the hips and hamstrings, as well as very loose clothing. Head-height kicks, while by no means impossible, are generally regarded as unnecessarily risky when defending yourself; if you want to attack the head it is usually easier to use the hands.

The Front Kick (Mae-geri)

This is the most basic kicking technique in ju-jitsu and probably the most useful for self-defence purposes. The kick is mechanically very simple; first lift your knee high, then straighten your leg, kicking out in front with your foot. There are basically two versions which use the ball of the foot as the striking area (or with shoes on, the toes); the snap kick, which is used as a distracting attack or as part of a combination to come within range for using hand techniques, and the more powerful thrust kick, which is intended to damage and incapacitate an attacker. Both kicks are normally used to the mid-section (stomach) of your attacker. A specialised front kick to the groin using the instep is known as *kin-geri*.

Fig 48–54 Kicks can be used for long distance counter-attacks, but also when close to an opponent and are especially effective when tori grabs uke's sleeve after blocking to prevent evasion. This illustration shows a front kick to the throat.

Fig 49   Uke grabs both tori's wrists.

Fig 50   Tori delivers a front kick to the groin to incapacitate his assailant.

The Side-Kick (Yoko-geri)

The side-kick can also be either a snap kick or a thrust kick. Its special uses are for tackling assailants who attack from the side; it allows the user to stand sideways-on to an attacker, presenting a smaller target area for frontal assault. The striking area is the outside edge (little-toe edge) of the foot or the outside edge of the heel. As with the front kick, the snap-kick version is normally delivered off the front leg and is less powerful than the thrust kick which, when delivered with the back foot, transmits the rotational power of the hips. As with most kicking techniques it should be practised keeping the supporting foot flat on the floor, not coming upon the toes. The knee should be lifted up first and as the kick is snapped or thrust out, the body leans to accommodate the shift in weight. *Yoko-geri* is particu-larly useful if you are forced to stamp on an attacker's knees in order to incapacitate him.

The Back Kick (Ushiro-geri)

This is a very powerful kick which can be used against attackers directly facing you. Turn around or spin, lifting your knee high and then thrust your leg out directly backwards. The striking area is the heel and the target area the pit of the stomach or mid-section of your assailant's body.

The Round-House Kick

The round-house kick in ju-jitsu tends to be used to attack the lower body, empha-sising the functional nature of kicking techniques for self-defence. Practising to kick head-height has numerous benefits, including improvements in flexibility,

Fig 51   The side kick to the knee.

Fig 52   The side kick to the ribs.

balance and control. For self-defence, however, most ju-jitsu instructors feel that high kicks are dangerously flashy, putting the kicker at greater risk than the same technique targeted at lower areas.

The Stamp Kick

This is an important technique for 'finishing off' an assailant on the floor; it functions in a manner similar to a back kick but is directed straight downwards. Stamping with the heel tends to be more effective than kicking in such situations and there is less danger of damage to your feet. The stamp kick can also be used to 'soften up' an attacker who grabs you from behind, by scraping your heel down his shins, stamping on to his instep or toes, all of which are painful techniques and are likely to remove his attention from keeping his hold on you.

Fig 53   The roundhouse kick to the solar plexus.

65

Fig 54 The hook kick to the jaw.

Knee Strikes (Hiza-geri)

These are extremely effective for close fighting. The knee can easily be driven into the groin in order to fell an attacker, or into the solar plexus or face if he is bending over, which might be the case if you are applying any of a number of locking techniques. The 'hair-grab' can also combine effectively with the knee to the face. The schoolboy dead-leg can also be used by driving the knee into the large nerve complex in the outer thigh to ensure that an assailant cannot give chase after you have escaped his clutches.

The Headbutt

This can be a particularly devastating close-range weapon; offensive and defensive strikes against frontal and rear attacks using the head are taught in many modern ju-jitsu schools. In the case of a frontal attack, the hard, bony area about two or three inches above the eyebrows is typically the striking area. The target area is generally the nose or cheek-bone. Bear in mind that the head, on average, is one-eighth of the body-weight and so quite a considerable amount of weight can be focused into a small area of hard bone, making it a very effective striking weapon.

7 Locking, Choking and Immobilisation Techniques

Unlike judo, where the only lock permitted within the rules of the sport are against the elbow, ju-jitsu locking techniques can be applied to any of the body's joints, including the fingers, wrists, knees, shoulders, ankles and neck. Many of the techniques of ju-jitsu for immobilising and throwing assailants using joint-locks can be found in other systems including aikido and sombo wrestling. In practice, joint-locks have various functions. They are useful for controlling an assailant through a painful and potentially damaging hold; they can force the strongest individuals off balance, making them easier to throw; they can be used to disarm assailants carrying weapons and to restrain and immobilise.

It is the usefulness of these locks for the purposes of restraining and immobilising that makes *kansetsu-waza* so appealing to policemen, prison guards and people in similar jobs, since they allow them to prevent violence without having to inflict it.

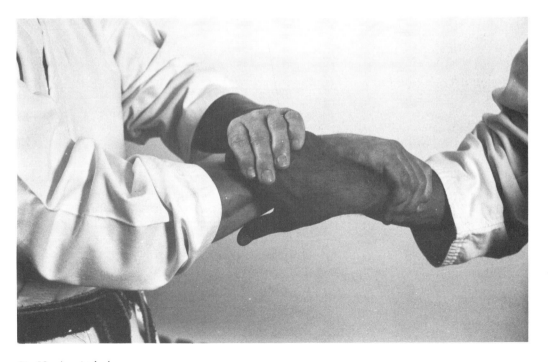

Fig 55   A wrist-lock.

In a situation demanding self-defence they can also be applied with the intention of causing immediate disabling injury to an assailant. Most locking techniques, if applied with force, will cause joint dislocation and muscle tearing at the very least, but even so when defending yourself you should only rarely employ them on their own; they are most effective when combined with strikes and throws.

The problem with using a joint-lock on an assailant if you are not a policeman or equivalent figure of authority performing a clearly defined function, is that once you have immobilised your attacker you then have to decide what to do with him. Unless you make a citizen's arrest and can persuade someone to contact the police you will, at some point, have to release your attacker. If he is prone to violence – more than likely if he attacked you in the first place – being kept in a painful and humiliating lock for any length of time is unlikely to have a calming effect and he may well attack you again if you release him; the human instinct for revenge, or 'getting even' is beyond rational explanation. For all you know, you may have a maniac in your grasp. For this reason it is considered to be better strategy to hit and run, leaving your attacker stunned and dazed, so allowing you a breathing space to get away.

Because many attacks begin with the assailant's hands coming into contact before any other part of his body, some form of wrist-lock is often the most appropriate technique with which to initiate a counter-attack. Frequently, controlling the wrist is the key to controlling your attacker's arm and, in turn, the attacker himself since it is a simple matter to consolidate a hold by moving up the arm with elbow- and shoulder-locks and so subdue him completely.

The principle of controlling an attacker by controlling his arm is germane to ju-jitsu. The reasons for this are both historical and functional. The people who designed the techniques of ju-jitsu were warriors, but so were their enemies and consequently both combatants were almost invariably armed. The weapons of the time, which were usually employed in hand-to-hand fighting on a battlefield, were the sword and dagger. In fact, the common fighting style of many warriors involved the use of two swords, one long (*katana*) and one shorter blade, (*waka-zashi*) as popularised by the master swordsman Miyamoto Musashi, author of the classic, *Go Rin No Sho (A Book of Five Rings).*

Out of this situation arose a requirement for dealing with the forms of attack likely from a man armed with a dagger or sword (although many techniques begin from the assumption that neither party has retained his sword). Accordingly the knife is the weapon that most frequently must be countered, while other techniques existed for completely unarmed combat. Most possible situations are covered, with pragmatism always being the overriding factor in the execution of attacks and defences, regardless of other variables. The *kime-no-kata* (*see* Chapter 10) covers a situation in which a potential attacker has his sword sheathed and advocates dealing with him by moving in and strangling before he can draw and use his weapon. The most interesting aspect of this particular *kata* is the dependence upon locking techniques for dealing with assailants armed with cutting and stabbing weapons. *Waki-gatame* and *hara-gatame* feature very prominently, although concepts relating to *hara* and *ki* are also influential in this respect.

The later *go-shin jutsu kata* supplements the *kime-no-kata* and the importance of controlling your opponent's arm is apparent there, too. There are two basic approaches adopted in the *kata* for dealing with knife attacks; one is to concentrate on the arm holding the knife and to lock it, the other is to keep well away from that hand and keep to the other side of the attacker's body, controlling the arm without the weapon, thereby not allowing him either to stab or cut with it.

It is important to realise that these techniques are not mere abstract ideas bunched together and called a *kata*; they have survived the test of time. They were devised by people trying to avoid being killed in combat; they were then and remain now essentially techniques of survival. Their effectiveness depends upon practising and using them in that same spirit.

The methods demonstrated in this chapter are best learned by practising them as single techniques before linking them into the more demanding self-defence routines illustrated. Once the basic techniques are mastered, however, the endless range of possibilities for combination techniques soon becomes clear.

Many of the locking techniques used in ju-jitsu are the same as those found in aikido and judo, although of course the wrist- and shoulder-locks are not allowed in judo. In aikido the locks are normally used either to throw or immobilise and the basic immobilisation techniques are: *ikkyo; nikyo; sankyo; yonkyo; gokyo; kote-gaeshi;* and *shiho-nage.* The latter two techniques can be used either to throw or to immobilise. In ju-jitsu the major difference is that *atemi-waza* can follow or precede these techniques, whereas the closest thing to an atemi-waza in modern aikido is to flick a hand at the attacker's eyes to distract him from your real intentions.

LOCKS

Wrist-Locks

Wrist-locking techniques are among the most useful of *kansetsu-waza* and are appropriate in a number of self-defence situations, ranging from your lapel being grabbed to knife attacks. The wrist is basically a hinge joint and generally has only a small degree of lateral movement, making torsional locking techniques particularly effective. The bones of the wrist are shaped in such a way that they inhibit lateral rotation and when forced out of alignment the pain caused is intense. It is a relatively simple matter to force someone to the floor when they are in such pain, but the choice of whether to inflict actual damage must remain with the defender. It is important to realise that techniques intended to lock the wrist are achieved by gripping the hand. When the wrist itself is gripped, for the purpose of performing a ju-jitsu or aikido technique, the intention is generally to lock the elbow or shoulder.

There are three basic ways to apply a wrist-lock: bend the hand at the wrist as if to make the fingers touch the inside of the forearm (*kote-gaeshi*); twist the hand in order to apply torsion on the wrist (*sankyo*); twist and bend the hand at the wrist causing torsional stress on the wrist and forearm (*nikyo* or *kote-mawashi*). In some cases these locks will start on the wrist and as the attacker wriggles and twists to relieve the pain the elbow and shoulder may become locked too, with little or no adaption on the part of the defender.

Because it is quite impossible to go into every technique in detail and in order to avoid repetition, only some of the locking techniques are actually illustrated in this chapter, but their variety and use can be

Fig 56–61   *A further example of a wrist-lock. In this illustration (Fig 56) uke grips both of tori's wrists.*

Fig 57   *Tori bends and rotates his left elbow as if doing* soto-uke.

Fig 58   Tori reaches across and grips uke's already twisted right hand with his own left hand.

Fig 59   Tori breaks uke's grip and applies both hands against uke's very twisted wrist.

Fig 60   Tori moves in circular fashion to his right while twisting to his left, twisting
uke painfully off balance and throwing him to the ground.

Fig 61   Tori follows up by kneeling on uke's head and hyperextending the elbow joint.

72

better understood by referring to Chapter 9 on self-defence, and in particular to the sections on gun and knife defences (pages 116–133) where they prove to be indispensable.

A version of *ikkyo* is illustrated in the sequence of photographs demonstrating a defence against your lapel being grabbed (Figs 74–7). Turning the hand to apply pressure on the wrist in this technique causes *uke* (the attacker) to reach from the shoulder straightening his arm to relieve the pain, an action *tori* (the defender) helps by taking a step backwards and twisting at the waist; this places the elbow in a perfect position to be locked. By attempting to alleviate the pressure on the elbow joint uke invariably has to drop his shoulder, ending up with all three joints of the arm twisted and locked. In this sequence tori has locked uke's elbow by putting his forearm on top of it, while retaining a grip on the hand and wrist. It is equally feasible, once the initial twisting action has made uke straighten the arm, for tori to release the left-hand grip on the wrist and grip the back of uke's arm just above the elbow. Tori can then walk forwards and push down causing uke to lie flat on the ground with his arm locked straight and pinned to the floor. One of the beauties of ju-jitsu is the breadth of response it allows to violent or aggressive situations.

Figs 62–7 The wrist-lock. Here (Fig 62) uke grips tori's lapel.

Fig 63 Tori responds by gripping uke's hand with his right hand in an over-the-top grip.

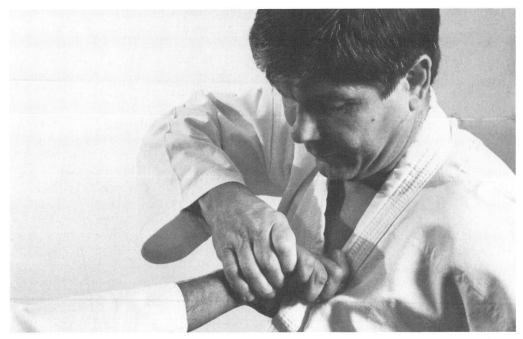

Fig 64   Note how tori controls uke's hand by gripping the fleshy part of the palm.

Fig 65   Uke applies a painful, controlling wrist-lock.

Fig 66   Tori forces uke's head down with a combined wrist and shoulder lock.

Fig 67   Tori consolidates his position with a combined wrist- and hammer-lock.

Figs 68–70 Defence against a lapel grab. Here (Fig 68) uke grips tori's jacket at the left lapel with his right hand.

Fig 69 Tori immediately reaches over with his right hand, gripping uke's hand from above at the same time as he grips his wrist from underneath with his left hand.

Fig 70 Turning uke's wrist in a clockwise direction and driving his elbow down on top of uke's straight arm he forces him off balance and controls him with a painful armlock. Applied with a jerk, this could break uke's arm.

Obtaining release from a grip on the wrist does not actually require any mastery of elaborate or difficult techniques. A straightforward punch on the jaw, knocking your assailant out will do it, but if the situation does not warrant such a drastic response you can simply twist free, always remembering to twist your wrists against the thumbs of the person who grabs you. As long as you make a circular movement with your hand before he can bring his weight to bear, you will invariably be able to break his grip, which may well dissuade many individuals from persisting with being physically aggressive. Compare these soft aikido-based techniques with the hard *atemi* responses to the same form of attack in Chapter 6. Remember, too, that both types of technique can easily be combined if a rapidly changing situation requires an increasingly violent response. The *kansetsu-waza* can

Fig 71–3   One of ju-jitsu's great strengths is the breadth of response it offers to all levels of violence. In the following sequence a defence against a wrist grab is illustrated. Here (Fig 71) uke grabs tori's wrists with an orthodox thumbs-on-the-inside grip.

Fig 72   Tori bends his arms and brings his hands inwards and upwards, so putting strain on uke's thumbs and wrists.

Fig 73   Uke is forced to release tori's wrists. No damage has been inflicted, but tori is free.

be applied to control or to damage and can easily be followed up with *atemi-waza* if necessary.

It is worth describing a couple of basic armlocks which are commonly used in judo at this point. *Waki-gatame* is one of the most effective of combined elbow- and shoulder-locks. Curiously enough, the most effective of contest armlocks, the *juji-gatame* or step-over armlock – which is very difficult to prevent once a skilled exponent gets on your back (as world champion Neil Adams demonstrated time and again, even winning his world title in 1981 by defeating Kase of Japan with it in the final) – is almost irrelevant to ju-jitsu. It makes no sense in a self-defence situation where the floor is likely to be hard and abrasive, having thrown an assailant, to follow up with this unless your intention is to break his arm and then get up.

Perhaps its only truly useful application occurs when you are actually on your back on the floor with an attacker between your legs. It can come in extremely useful in these circumstances, particularly if the attacker is trying to throttle you, but even then, there are other more appropriate techniques (*see* 'Ground Techniques' in Chapter 9, page 133). *Waki-gatame* is undeniably useful and despite the fact that it can only be applied against the elbow joint in judo matches and even in practice, in a ju-jitsu context the shoulder is also fair game. The degree to which it is a shoulder-lock is determined by the flexibility of the person being locked. Often the strong but bulky mesomorph (someone with a compact, muscular body-build) will be more vulnerable to such techniques, particularly so if he or she has a limited range of movement as a result of having

Fig 74–7 This sequence shows another defence against a lapel grab. In this illustration (Fig 74) uke grabs tori's left lapel with his right hand.

Fig 75   Tori responds by grabbing uke's right hand from above with his right hand.

Fig 76   Tori turns uke's hand clockwise through 180 degrees until the thumb is pointing down to the ground and the edge of the little finger points to the ceiling. Tori applies painful lateral pressure to uke's wrist joint by levering down on the wrist and up on the hand, forcing him to his knees.

Fig 77   If necessary tori can follow up with a downward elbow strike to dislocate uke's shoulder.

developed excessively bulky muscles. *Waki-gatame* involves gripping your assailant's wrist with both hands and turning against his arm, pulling it straight across the front of your chest and trapping the back of his upper arm under your armpit. This allows you to press your body-weight against his upper arm, immobilising it and to pull on the wrist with both hands, hyperextending the elbow joint (bending it the wrong way) which is extremely painful. This technique is particularly easy to apply against people with strong arms who attempt to push with their arms stretched out rigidly, either standing up or fighting on the ground. Standing *hara-gatame* (*see* the *kime-no-kata* technique of *tsukkomi* in Chapter 10) is very similar to *waki-gatame* to the beginner but the points of contact are in fact very different. In *waki-gatame* the upper arm is under the armpit and the elbow pulled up against the side of the chest. In *hara-gatame* the arm is held lower, the back of the elbow being pulled into the stomach below the navel. The ground-fighting version of *hara-gatame* makes special use of the legs and this helps distinguish the two techniques.

Locking techniques to the elbow joint fall into two basic groups: straight armlocks, such as *ude-gatame* and *waki-gatame*, in which the arm is pulled straight and direct pressure is applied against the elbow-joint, so hyperextending it; and bent armlocks such as the *ude-garami* or 'figure four' which stress the joint laterally. Often it is easier to lock the elbow by twisting the wrist first and the pain involved makes it very easy to force or even throw uke to the floor.

Fig 78–84 *Locks can be effectively combined with throws as this sequence illustrates. First of all (Fig 78) uke grabs tori's lapel.*

Fig 79 *Uke attempts to punch tori in the face, but tori blocks with a rising knife hand.*

Fig 80 *Tori immediately grabs uke's right wrist with his left hand and brings his right arm up inside uke's left arm.*

Fig 81 *Bringing his arm over and down behind uke's triceps muscle tori applies a bent armlock (ude-garami).*

Fig 82 *With the armlock already on tori passes uke's right arm into his right hand.*

Fig 83 *Tori has uke completely controlled and hooks uke's left leg away tripping him with ko-soto-gake.*

82

Fig 84   Tori can at this stage drop uke, or follow up with an additional wrist lock.

Leg-locks

Leg-locks have always been an important part of ju-jitsu training and still play an important role in some modern combat sports such as sombo wrestling. A leg-lock is a potentially devastating technique since it can effectively incapacitate the most powerful of attackers. However, they do have the disadvantage that they can normally only be applied in ground-work fighting. An exception to this occurs when an attacker attempts to kick and you are able to grab his leg and throw him. The throw can be immediately followed up with a leg-lock, but the rationale for using such a technique must be to render him incapable of standing, perhaps to allow you to get to your feet and away.

As a general rule, legs are stronger than

arms and many armlocks exploit this fact. The legs do have weaknesses, though, and both the ankle and the knee are susceptible to locking techniques.

Although the leg-lock shown is one derived from Russian sombo wrestling, the classic ju-jitsu leg-lock is *ashi-garami*, or the 'leg entanglement'. This is a technique unsurprisingly long since banned in judo dojos because it effectively twists the knee. Bearing in mind the number of judo players who have suffered knee injuries by accident, permitting such techniques in *ne-waza* would doubtless greatly add to the damage.

The sombo-based technique can be considered as a possible follow-up in the sequence of photographs showing a defence against a kick. This sequence could just as easily run as follows: the attacker kicks to the defender's groin; the defender

83

Fig 85–94   Combinations of leg-grabs and footsweeps are particularly effective against kicks, because it is always more difficult to maintain balance on one leg than two. Here (Fig 85) uke attacks with a front kick to tori's lower abdomen. Fig 86   Tori side-steps the kick with a simple tai-sabaki (body movement) and catches uke's leg at the ankle.

Fig 87   Tori grabs uke's collar with his right hand at the back of his neck. This is a variable within the technique. If tori wants to control uke's fall he should grip some part of his gi, but in a street attack he could simply make a palm-heel strike to the face if he wanted to throw uke on the back of his head. Tori rotates through 180 degrees to unbalance uke completely and then sweeps his supporting leg away with an o-uchi-gari type action. Fig 88   Tori throws uke to the ground.

Fig 89　How tori follows up depends, to some
extent, upon how badly hurt uke is and the position
in which his legs finish. The first follow-up sees
tori spread uke's legs by using his knees . . .

Fig 90　. . . and then punch to the testicles.

Fig 91　Alternatively he could step straight
between uke's legs and side-stamp kick to his throat.

Fig 92　The third option involves going into
groundwork; tori grabs uke's knee in a leg lock.

Fig 93   Tori kneels on uke's groin to 'soften him up'.

side-steps, catches the leg under his arm and executes a leg-sweep take-down. He immediately follows up with a stamping kick to the groin and 'sits into' a crippling ankle-lock to incapacitate his assailant, completely.

With this technique the force is applied by trapping the foot under the upper arm and levering up with the back, transmitting power through the cutting edge of the wrist, which puts pressure on the insertion of the Achilles tendon. Apply this technique with care in practice as it is deceptively powerful and can easily result in dislocation of the ankle.

Finger-locks

Finger-locks are quite essential ju-jitsu techniques since they apply the defender's force against the aggressor's weakest

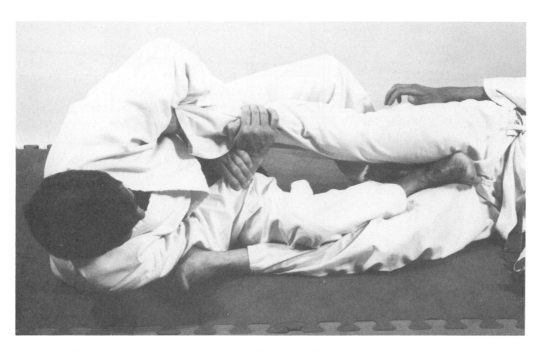

Fig 94   He then stands on the groin and rolls to the floor where he applies a leg lock on the ankle.

point. This sort of technique is invariably branded 'dirty fighting' by physically stronger bullies who are only happy to fight as long as the odds are stacked in their favour. Snapping and twisting fingers is an important branch of ju-jitsu, particularly for the young, the old and women, since it gives them an important chance to inflict serious damage on attackers who are likely to be physically stronger. Finger twisting is particularly useful against strangling and choking attacks which are often used in sexual assaults. Generally speaking, the little fingers are the weakest and even a very weak person can, with the element of surprise, inflict painful damage on the strongest of men.

STRANGLES AND CHOKES

Strangles and chokes, collectively called *shime-waza*, are not *kansetsu-waza*, but are often treated as neck-locks in books on ju-jitsu. Many of these techniques can easily be turned into neck-locks, but their intention in their normal form is to cause choking and/or unconsciousness.

The neck is a particularly vulnerable part of the human body and susceptible to a number of forms of attack. Chokes and strangleholds are apparently very similar, but in fact are considerably different both in application and intention. The strangle cuts off the blood supply to the brain whereas the choke prevents air from reaching the lungs. The well applied strangle is rarely painful and has the effect of rendering victims unconscious, often without their even being aware of it. The choke, on the other hand, is highly unpleasant causing both gagging and panic, and is most effective as a painful controlling technique or if used in warfare as a method of killing an enemy. If applied forcefully, choke holds can cause severe damage to the windpipe and throat by crushing the trachea. Chokes must be considered as more dangerous than strangles in this respect and in training neither should ever be applied with a jerking action since this greatly increases the danger of causing damage to the neck.

The danger inherent in the stranglehold ought not to be underestimated; brain damage and death can both result from these actions.

Rear Strangles

A rear strangle, as the name suggests, is one applied from behind. Once it is in place a rear strangle is one of the most effective of methods for rendering an attacker unconscious. Perhaps most pertinent of all, when defending yourself, is that it is very difficult for an attacker to inflict any injury on you if you are on his back strangling him. Basically rear strangles are of two types; those that use the jacket and those in which the arm encircles the neck. This latter type does not require an assailant to be wearing a jacket. The effectiveness of jacket-type strangles such as *kata-ha-jime* or *okuri-eri-jime* can be enhanced or reduced substantially by the kind of material from which the jacket is made; some fabrics, such as silk, can have an effect almost like a cheese-wire.

There are, of course, some other important considerations that must not be overlooked. The first of these is to ensure that the assailant is kept off balance. The methods used to ensure this is so will be determined by the relative heights of the attacker and defender. Taller people need only bend their attacker's head back, arching their body to keep him off balance; the effect is similar to that of being hanged. Shorter exponents may need to kick or stamp on the back of a taller attacker's knees to get him down to a manageable level.

Facing Strangles

Facing strangles are an important area well worth studying. They can be particularly useful for shielding yourself in the case of multiple attack. Any of the three basic frontal strangles (*nami, gyaku* or *kata-juji-jime*) can be quickly applied using your attacker's jacket and you can keep him between yourself and his accomplices until he is unconscious. These methods can also provide a quick means of escape from becoming entangled in a struggle on the ground and can be readily applied either from underneath or on top of your assailant. They are particularly effective if ever you find yourself in a situation where someone manages to get on top of you on the ground. Being the 'underdog' position clearly aids the effectiveness of such strangles. Experiment in training with a partner of similar skill and strength. Both of you should have your hands in position for the same strangle, one on top and one underneath before a third person claps as a signal to start applying the strangle. Try all the strangles and alternate between being on top and underneath; you should find that the person who is underneath almost invariably forces a submission from the opponent. Try it and see for yourself, but remember that you will be unable to tap with your hands to signal an effective technique, so be ready to strike the mat with your feet.

Neck-locks and Spine-locks

Neck- and spine-locks are potentially lethal techniques which, if applied with excessive

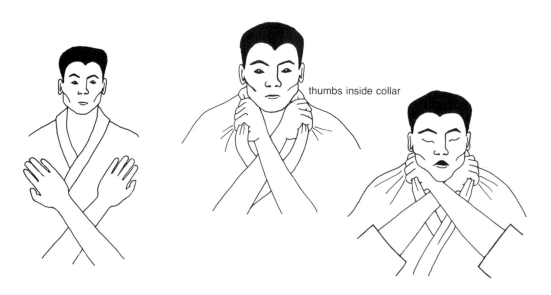

thumbs inside collar

Fig 95 Hand positions for strangles:
(a) Nami-juji-jime;

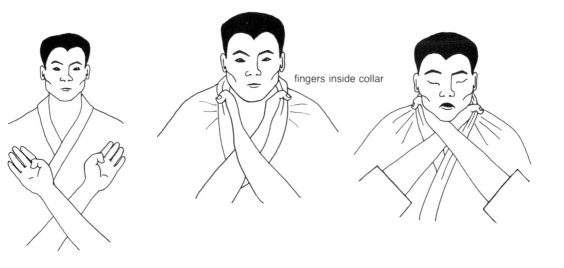

fingers inside collar

(b) Gyaku-juji-jime;

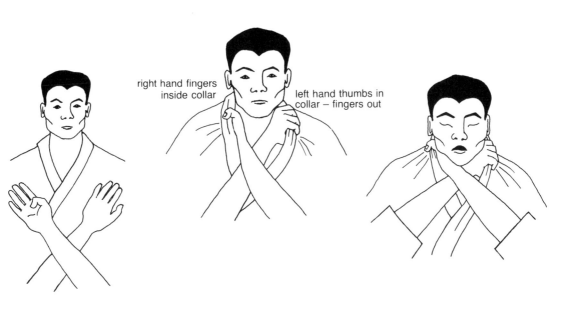

right hand fingers
inside collar

left hand thumbs in
collar – fingers out

(c) Kata-juji-jime;

force, can leave an assailant paralysed. These, therefore, must be practised and used only with a great deal of care. Many opportunities to apply such techniques occur in ground fighting. In standing work there are some basic applications of neck-locks which allow sufficient control of the assailant – this will let the jujitsuka bring the assailant to the ground well under control.

8 Throwing Techniques: Nage-waza

The throwing techniques of ju-jitsu are the most varied and extensive of any martial art. One of the reasons for this is they were originally fighting techniques which have evolved from warfare rather than from sport. Because most enemies tended to be wearing armour, the effectiveness of striking techniques was limited. This led to a wide range of hand-to-hand techniques being developed for close combat – with throwing and grappling in order to disarm and immobilise an enemy becoming particularly vital.

Another factor which strongly affected the development of techniques was the type of weapon the warrior was likely to find himself confronting, namely swords, knives and spears. The control of the arm holding the weapon was favoured as the way to deal with a stabbing attack and the existence of techniques such as *hara-gatame* and *waki-gatame* can be attributed to the need to disarm swordsmen, or at least warriors armed with knives.

The wearing of armour and the muddy, slippery nature of most battlefields also explains the existence of a surprisingly elaborate range of sacrifice throws. *Sutemi-waza* are regarded as inherently perilous techniques in combat sports such as judo and karate, since throwers sacrifice their own balance and upright position in the hope of downing their opponent. On a blood-soaked, muddy battlefield, however, where keeping one's balance was excessively difficult it was important not to go to the ground at a disadvantage and *sutemi-waza* provided a means of turning the tables just before impact, and so getting on top of an enemy.

There are five basic groups of throwing techniques in judo. These are: *ashi-waza* (foot throws); *koshi-waza* (hip throws); *te-waza* (hand throws); *sutemi-waza* (back sacrifice throws); and *yoko-sutemi-waza* (side sacrifice throws). The Kodokan system groups these in sets of eight throws and calls them the *go-kyo*. There are many more throws commonly practised and witnessed in competitions that are not included in the *go-kyo*, many are generically classified as 'take-downs' and do not have a proper name. Ju-jitsu, however, has many more throws than those that comprise the *go-kyo* and the unnamed throws found in judo. Many of these techniques do not fit into any of the above categories. Particularly difficult to categorise are the leg entanglements that are prohibited techniques in contest judo and some of those throws deriving from aikido techniques. Unlike contemporary sport judo where it is prohibited to precede a throw by a blow or to throw from a joint-lock, ju-jitsu permits any and all actions which contribute to defeating an assailant. One consequence of this is that techniques must be practised with greater care and exponents must develop great skill. Many ju-jitsu techniques would lead to disqualification in a judo or karate tournament as they have nothing to do with these contests.

All throwing practice is carried out in a spirit of mutual co-operation and partners offer only minimal resistance. The reasoning behind this is that if a throw is used, in reality it will be preceded by a distracting blow or combined with a locking technique that will make resistance impossible. Ju-jitsu teachers traditionally regarded the art as an elitist activity which could be studied only by a few select groups and one of the major reasons for its efficacy was the secrecy surrounding its techniques. Indeed, different schools or *ryu* had their own specialities which students were forbidden by patriarchal *senseis* from divulging to anyone outside the *ryu*. Modern ju-jitsu schools are quite different in this respect, although the feeling of becoming part of a large family, with the *sensei* as its head, is very strong in many dojos. The techniques are no longer kept secret and are freely exchanged between students of the modern form of the art. The more knowledge available the better it is for all concerned.

The arbitrary classification of throws into groups is good for the purposes of learning as it is a convenient method of preserving technical knowledge, but it can be misleading for the novice. The fact that a *tai-otoshi* is classed as a hand throw does not mean, for instance, that the thrower uses only his hands in the execution of the technique. All throws are complicated feats of co-ordination requiring the effective utilisation of the power of the whole body. Head, hands, feet, hips and trunk operate together in harmony to perform even the most basic footsweep. The more effective the individual's co-ordination is, the more effective the throw will be.

The best way to develop co-ordination is to perform numerous repetitions of the throw. This means many 'turn-ins' (*uchi-komi*) and completions (*nagekomi*), ensuring that you perfect the technique before trying it at full speed. Initially speed should not be a major concern, although frequently it is easier to perform a throw if the movements are made fairly quickly. Break the technique down into its component parts, concentrating on individual elements of the skill, such as the action of the hands or the positioning of the head or the steps involved in the footwork. When the basic body positioning and mechanics of the throw are right, train to combine skill and speed by making big complete movements, paying particular attention to finishing. When throwing skill is sufficiently well developed it is very easy to add locking techniques and subtle refinements, but it is essential to perfect the basic throw before embroidering the technique with little extra details.

The throws in ju-jitsu are executed according to the same dynamic theory in judo (and to a lesser extent aikido), depending upon the extent to which the teacher advocates the development and use of *ki*. Basically, any throwing action must involve taking a grip (*kumikata*), breaking the balance of the person to be thrown (*kuzushi*) and actually completing the throw (*kake*). The person being thrown can be either standing still or moving when thrown: if standing still when the throw is attempted, the force utilised will be entirely the thrower's. The thrower has to create the impetus (*ikioi*) to effect the technique, which requires strength. If the opponent can be thrown whilst moving it is possible to use his or her momentum (*hazumi*). This greatly increases the force of the throw because the impact is a result of the combined energies of the thrower and the 'thrown'. This requires a more subtle level of skill and has to take into account other variables.

Fig 96–100   Defence against a front strangle (2). Here (Fig 96) tori grips uke's right arm with his left hand, grabbing the crook of his elbow from underneath.

Fig 97   Tori strikes uke at the base of the nose with a reverse knife hand.

Fig 98   Tori forces uke off balance by forcing his head back, pressing the edge of his hand (by his little finger) against the base of uke's nose and simultaneously pulls on his right elbow with his left hand.

Fig 99   Tori throws uke to the floor and kneels on his head.

Fig 100   Tori can, if necessary, finish uke off with and armlock and a stamping kick to the head.

Fig 101-6 *Defence against a front strangle. In this illustration (Fig 101) uke grabs tori's neck and attempts to throttle him.*

Fig 102 *Tori responds by pushing down on uke's left elbow and up on the right one and stepping in to uke.*

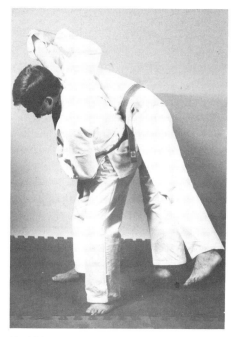

Fig 103 *Tori spins into a* tsuri-komi-goshi *(a lifting pulling hip throw) and jacks uke up on his hips.*

Fig 104 *Tori straightens his legs and bends at the waist, dipping his head to fling uke over.*

Fig 105   *Tori retains control of uke as he hits the floor by maintaining his grip on uke's wrist.*

Fig 106   *If necessary tori can follow up with a punch to the head.*

ASHI-WAZA

There are a number of different *ashi-waza*, but basically these throws involve using your foot or lower leg to sweep your opponents off their feet and throw them to the ground. Skilful exponents of *ashi-waza* can throw an assailant without even taking a hold, purely by using a fast sweeping action of the leg, timed to perfection. However, it is almost always desirable to grip with at least one hand in order to maintain control of an assailant and, of course, when practising with a partner it makes his or her fall considerably less painful if you provide some support.

There are various types of *ashi-waza* and a distinction needs to be drawn between sweeping *ashi-waza* and reaping, or scything techniques. Of all the throwing techniques the sweeping *ashi-waza* are those that rely most heavily on perfect timing and footwork; they cannot be forced as hip and hand throws can. Of course the reaping leg throws, *o-soto-gari* and the like, can be beefed up if stiff resistance is encountered.

One of the great advantages of *ashi-waza* is that those performing the technique do not need to commit or risk themselves very much at all. Other advantages are that the technique attacks low, well below the level of defensive awareness of the untrained assailant and that it takes effect with a suddenness akin to slipping on a patch of ice or a banana skin. There is little more disconcerting than being face to face with an opponent one moment and flat on your back, winded the next.

Figs 107–11 Throws can be preceded by locking techniques to good effect, as in this sequence. Here (Fig 107) uke grabs tori's lapel intending to punch him.

Fig 108 Tori responds by immediately applying ude-gatame. Pressure on the elbow causes uke to stand on tip-toe in an effort to relieve the pain.

Fig 109 If tori is taller this makes uke easy to sweep with ashi-barai.

Fig 110 If Tori is shorter than uke he may prefer to throw him with o-soto-gari.

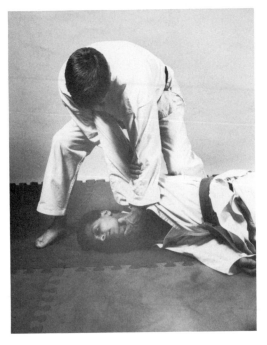

Fig 111   If necessary tori can finish uke off with a pinch choke.

For beginners trying to work out how best to co-ordinate their body movements to perform good *ashi-waza* there is a simple formula which reduces any technique to three basic considerations: pull up with the hands; sweep away the foundations; pull down with the hands. This, like all such formulae, is an oversimplification, but can prove useful for grasping the essential idea. In ju-jitsu an armlock will quite often be used to raise an attacker to his toes, making it easier to sweep his legs away, especially when the pain is distracting him so that he is focusing his attention on the joint being locked.

Te-waza (hand techniques) are among some of the most impressive and spectacular of throws and have a major advantage in that they can be achieved without sacrificing your balance by standing on one leg, as is the case with many leg- and

hip-throws. The shoulder-throws which involve throwing your partner or assailant over your head, belong to this group and like the *tai-otoshi* (body drop) are very popular with smaller exponents needing to throw bigger assailants.

Hip-throws are the core of most forms of wrestling and score very highly in judo competition. One of the few drawbacks with using a hip-throw is that an assailant may cling on to you and drag you to the ground with him as he falls. If you are a heavyweight this may prove to be a very unpleasant experience for him, but should you be lighter than he, you could be putting yourself in a situation in which he might be able to take advantage of his superior size and weight. On the positive side the effects of a hip-throw can be quite shattering; indeed such techniques are very difficult to anticipate or stop for those without the necessary knowledge. Hip-throws also rely much less upon the assailant wearing a jacket or other long-sleeved clothing than other techniques since it is a simple matter to grab the wrist; your other arm can easily go under the armpit and around the back as in *o-goshi* or alternatively around his neck as in *kube-nage*.

Sacrifice techniques are of limited value for self-defence, especially when hard surfaces are likely to have replaced mats. They should only really be used by real experts and even they are severely limited in their application. They should be last-resort methods for dealing with an opponent, but are worthy of serious study (especially by higher grades) as there are circumstances under which there is no other option but to use one. If a sacrifice technique fails there is always the possibility of following up with an appropriate strangle or locking technique for which the thrower will be ideally positioned.

Figs 112–18 One of the most basic ju-jitsu throwing techniques is the hip throw. The version is performed against a punching attack. Initially (Fig 112) tori and uke are both in the same fighting stance.

Fig 113 Uke steps in and punches to tori's head, but tori blocks with a knife hand. (The knife hand makes grabbing uke's sleeve for the forthcoming throw easier than it would be with a closed fist block.)

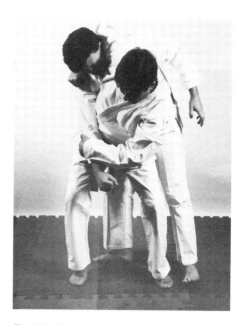

Fig 114 Tori grabs uke's sleeve and immediately encircles uke's neck with his right arm.

Fig 115 Tori turns in on uke with kube-nage, the neck throw, ensuring that his centre of gravity is well under uke's. Note the pull with both arms and the bent-knee position.

99

Fig 116 Tori bends forwards, driving back with his hips and pulling over with his arms, turning his head as he does so. Uke goes flying over tori's hip.

Fig 117 Uke crashes to the ground and tori keeps hold of his wrist.

Fig 118 Tori finishes uke off with a punch to the head.

To grasp the intricacies of throwing technique properly and develop genuinely skilful throwing abilities the student of ju-jitsu must practise *randori* (free play). If you go to a club where there is never any *randori*, find a judo club in your area and go along once or twice a week. There you will find out if you can really throw and fall – or not. *Randori* is essential for the sake of realism if for no other reason. You may feel you are handicapping yourself by not employing your full range of ju-jitsu techniques, but you will undoubtedly benefit from the experience. By the same token, it is equally worth while to spar with boxers and karateka from time to time, to gain an indication of the relative speed, power and sheer toughness of other martial artists. If you visit other dojo, go with an open mind and go there to learn.

Figs 119–24   *The importance of* ju *(flexibility or adaptability) in a judo contest. This photograph illustrates (Fig 119) also the remarkable awareness and reactions of top-flight judo fighters (this example is from the Seoul Olympic games). The thrower stretches his opponent out with the* uchi-mata *(inner thigh throw) and commits his body-weight to the attack.*

Fig 120   *Both players begin to fall.*

Fig 121 Waza-ari, *a half point score, is awarded because, despite having impetus, the thrower has been unable to put his opponent flat on his back – even though using a* maki-komi *action and landing on top of his opponent.*

Fig 122 The thrower allows the built-up momentum to carry him over his opponent's body.

Fig 123   As he rolls over, the thrower has released his grip on his opponent's sleeve and switched his hand to the crotch of his trousers. At the same time, he has stopped the roll by propping out his right leg and has disentangled his left leg to land in a holding position – yoko-shiho-gatame.

Fig 124   The grip is secure and the count begins. Twenty-five seconds later the thrower has won by wasari-awasete-ippon.

103

Treat all members of the dojo with respect, especially the *sensei*, and do not under any circumstances challenge anyone; such behaviour is strictly for the Bruce Lee movies. A final word of advice on this matter; it is generally a good idea to go along and watch what you will be letting yourself in for rather than diving in at the deep end. Best of all, go with a friend. (Throws combined with armlocks were also covered in Chapter 7, on locking techniques.)

The *go-kyo no-waza* (exposition of throwing techniques) was set down in 1895 as the definitive body of throwing techniques by the Kodokan. It comprises five groups of eight techniques and it is recommended that the throws be learned in order, if mastery is to be achieved. Since then other throws have been added to the repertoire of formally recognised techniques grouped under the title *shimmeisho no-waza*. These number seventeen, but a number of throwing techniques still remain unclassified. In the absence of a formal compilation of jujitsu *nage-waza* it is convenient to use the *go-kyo* as a point of reference. The techniques of the *shimmeisho no-waza* are listed for the same reason. When a technique has a name it is easier to remember and, to quote one of the old masters; 'Memory is not merely a quiescent, passive function; that which is not remembered every day is forgotten. We must remember or things become lost.'

The Go-kyo no-waza

First group
Deashi-harai	advancing footsweep
Hiza-guruma	knee wheel
Sasae Tsuri Komi Ashi	propping, lifting, pulling ankle throw
Uki-goshi	floating hip throw

O-soto-gari	major outer reap
Ogoshi	major hip throw
Ouchi-gari	major inner reap
Seoi-nage	shoulder throw

Second group
Kosoto-gari	minor outer reap
Kouchi-gari	minor inner reap
Koshi-guruma	hip wheel
Tsurikomi-goshi	lifting, pulling hip throw
Okuri Ashi Harai	sliding footsweep
Tai-otoshi	body drop
Harai-goshi	sweeping hip throw
Uchi Mata	inner thigh throw

Third group
Kosoto-gake	minor outer hook
Tsuri-goshi	drawing hip throw
Yoko-otoshi	side drop
Ashi-guruma	ankle wheel
Hane-goshi	springing hip throw
Harai-tsurikomi-ashi	lifting, pulling footsweep
Tomoe-nage	circle throw
Kata-guruma	shoulder wheel

Fourth group
Sumi-gaeshi	corner throw
Tani-otoshi	valley drop
Hane-makikomi	springing, winding throw
Sukui-nage	scooping throw
Utsuri-goshi	changing hip throw
Oguruma	major wheel
Soto-makikomi	outer winding throw
Uki-otoshi	floating drop

Fifth group
Osoto-guruma	major outer wheel
Uki-waza	floating technique
Yoko-wakare	side separation
Yoko-guruma	side wheel
Ushiro-goshi	rear hip throw

Ura-nage	rear throw
Sumi-otoshi	corner drop
Yoko-gake	side hook

The Shimmeisho no-waza

Morote-gari, kuchiki-taoshi, kibisu-gaeshi, uchi-mata-sukashi, dakiage, tsubame-gaeshi, osoto-gaeshi, hane-goshi-gaeshi, uchi-mata-gaeshi, kani-basami, kawazu-gake, osoto-makikomi, uchi-mata-makikomi, harai-makikomi.

It has often been said that martial arts are basically conservative activities resistant to change; this is indeed clearly the case. A whole host of techniques are being practised in judo dojos around the world, and even used in Olympic competition, but are not yet officially recognised by the Kodokan (where judo was founded). Many do not have Japanese names, largely because they were not originated in Japan but some do, such as *obi-tori-gaeshi* and *hikkomi-gaeshi*. The relevance of this to the student of ju-jitsu is acute; in many senses judo is the latest form of two of the more important aspects of ju-jitsu, throwing and grappling, so it is important to keep in touch with technical developments.

9 Self-defence Techniques

One technique mastered is worth a thousand sampled.

Away from the battlefield the only instance in which ju-jitsu techniques should ever be applied outside the dojo is when you need to defend yourself against violent attack. The requirements for success in a real situation are probably eighty per cent psychological and twenty per cent physical. Essentially it is a straightforward business of assessing the problem and then taking the appropriate action. When taking this action it is vital to be one hundred per cent committed to it, as well as to avoid being over-sophisticated. Sort out the situation as quickly and as directly as possible with the least risk to yourself and those who matter to you. There are no prizes for style; all that counts is judging the situation correctly and being effective.

Judging the situation accurately can often be the most difficult aspect of defending yourself; you must be able to recognise and anticipate threats, to know when to react and retain sufficient presence of mind not to over-react. A further consideration is speed – not just the speed at which you perform, how fast you move or hit, but how quickly you react to bring the situation to a conclusion. Decisiveness is crucial.

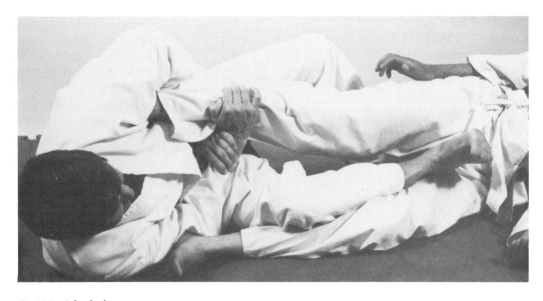

Fig 125 A leg-lock.

106

It is often said that there are no new techniques in martial arts, that everything that can be done has already been done, that there are no secrets in the martial arts any longer and so their effectiveness is reduced. This may or may not be true, but what is certain is that techniques come in and out of fashion and are forgotten or distorted. Modern ju-jitsu is fortunate as a system in that it does allow for the discovery and learning of new techniques; it remains an open-ended training for self-defence. Anything which helps ju-jitsu students or improves their chances when defending themselves may be considered worthy of study.

One point which inevitably has to be considered is how much time and energy, in terms of training, the development of a particular technique merits. The jumping, spinning reverse crescent kick or the axe-kick so popular in taekwondo and some styles of karate are undoubtedly spectacularly effective and impressive kicks. They are also highly specialised and extremely difficult to learn, as well as being extremely limited in their application. Ju-jitsu practitioners train to develop all-round, usable self-defence skills and must consider the value, in real terms, of training to add such techniques to their repertoire.

There is an immense difference between sport fighting and self-defence; practical efficiency and realism are the hallmarks of genuine ju-jitsu techniques; they are functional as opposed to flashy. Basic ju-jitsu, as practised in a good dojo, needs little modification for self-defence purposes, it is simply a question of performing the same techniques with the intention of causing injury – if necessary. There is a school of thought which maintains that ju-jitsu is the ultimate in self-defence; certainly a person thoroughly trained in

ju-jitsu can be a formidable adversary. Although it has developed into an activity that provides the practitioner with benefits far beyond a simple method of self-defence it should never be forgotten that ju-jitsu originated as a fighting system used on the battlefield. The application of ju-jitsu is nothing less than weaponless warfare and a situation that demands self-defence, depending on the circumstances, should be considered just that.

There are so many ways that one person can attack another that the only means of training effectively for self-defence is to develop the ability to react instantaneously to aggressive behaviour. The wide variety of methods taught in ju-jitsu gives the student the best possible range of techniques for dealing with almost every conceivable situation. It is also the case that a grasp of ju-jitsu methods allows the potential victim to respond with a precise degree of force required in a given situation – from a painful but harmless wrist-lock to potentially fatal strikes and strangle techniques which can be utilised in life-threatening situations. It is also important, however, to develop a *tokui-waza* (a speciality) – something you can rely upon to help you deal with an attacker. It may be a punch, a kick, a throw or a lock, but you must be able to perform at least one thing so well that you feel it could work on anyone.

Specific techniques are also taught in ju-jitsu for dealing with armed attacks, the weapons ranging from clubs and knives to guns. Sometimes, however, the weapons carried by an assailant are not very easily identifiable unless you are used to looking for them. Many men wear heavy gold rings on their fingers. In most cases they are just that, but in others they are worn specifically for their value as legal knuckledusters. Shoes and boots with

Figs 126–32   Knife defence (1). Here (Fig 126) tori is in left free fighting stance and uke is threatening his face with a knife.

Fig 127   Uke lunges with the knife; tori side-steps and blocks with his right hand.

Fig 128   Tori grabs uke's right wrist with his right hand and hits him in the side of the jaw with a palm-heel strike turning his head away from the knife.

108

Fig 129   Tori then reaches over uke's right arm at the crook of the elbow
and reaches under to grab his own right wrist.

Fig 130   Tori bends uke's arm, which is now in a wrist-lock, back in
towards him so that the knife is at his throat.

Fig 131 *With this leverage it is an easy matter for tori to step behind uke's right leg with his right leg and trip him to the ground.*

Fig 132 *Tori follows up with a knee-drop to the head of uke and forces him to drop the knife by applying more pressure with the wrist-lock.*

steel toe-caps are another hidden threat, capable of turning an ordinary kick into a potentially lethal blow. In the case of women, stiletto heels can, of course, do shocking damage as can the brick in the handbag which hits you on the head when the trouble-maker's girlfriend decides to help him out. Dangers are not always obvious and there are, sadly, some real connoisseurs of exotic violence walking the streets. Razor-blades stitched into lapels to cut the hands of anyone trying to grab them, razor-blades in caps to slash at the face or hands, the iron bar in the rolled-up newspaper, the bottle of beer in the jacket pocket, the ammonia in the nasal spray, the modelling knife, the artist's scalpel, the pool cue, the baseball bat in the boot of the car; the list is interminable,

the inventory of weapons in the urban arsenal seemingly boundless.

Facing an individual armed with a recognisable weapon, you are instantly aware of a new level of violence. An irksome drunk and an armed mugger are wholly different propositions, the former may be humoured, side-stepped, even ignored, without ever reaching the level of becoming a violent threat; the latter should put you in top gear as soon as you are aware of his existence. Whenever weapons are involved, you must immediately become one hundred per cent alert; there is no warming up, no second chances. Whatever you do, make it count.

Whilst the knife and the club may be the commonest weapons among delinquents in the United Kingdom, other countries have different associated weapons. In North America the hand-gun is commonplace and is frequently employed in muggings and robberies. Firearms obviously represent a different level of threat and negate even the most highly trained individual's fighting skills – except in very close-range situations. Defences against hand-guns other than those in this chapter are dealt with in the *go-shin jutsu kata* in Chapter 10.

Two-against-one training as preparation for multiple assault is an important component of training in many ju-jitsu dojo. The days of one-against-one fighting are long gone and if you are attacked in the street it is more than likely that it will be by more than one assailant. Muggers operate in twos and threes and in extreme cases large gangs beat and rob individuals in crowds (this latest phenomenon of modern urban violence is known as steaming).

One of the major problems with preparing a ju-jitsu student for the harsh reality of a street attack is that of contact. It is all very well practising innumerable techniques against co-operative training partners acting out hypothetical scenarios, but the real thing can be very different. Boxers, judo players or contact karate fighters who need to defend themselves have a very good idea of what will happen when they unleash a certain technique in the course of defending themselves. Full power techniques employed against fully resisting opponents are an integral part of these modern combat sports. Ju-jitsu students who have only ever practised techniques and have no actual experience of

Fig 133–8 Multiple attack (2). This (Fig 133) shows tori being attacked by two assailants. One grabs his wrists from behind and the other grabs his lapel, intending to punch him in the face.

Fig 134   Tori kicks the man in front of him in the groin before he throws the punch.

Fig 135   Tori then stamps back against his other assailant's knee and turns to face him, breaking his grip as he does so.

112

Fig 136 *Tori grabs his wrists and turns in for cross-arm* seoi-nage.

Fig 137 *Tori throws uke to the ground.*

Fig 138 *Uke cannot resist or his arms will be broken as the fall is a heavy one.*

fighting are at a disadvantage. The street is a much harder environment than the dojo, in every sense of the word.

The punch-bag, focus pads and target mitts are indispensable to the development of accurate and effective hitting power and to allow trainees to feel the effect (or lack of it) of their techniques.

Many ju-jitsu coaches are reluctant to introduce their students to the more physically punishing aspects of training for fear of losing them. Obviously, it is not a good idea for beginners to practise contact, but probably by brown belt, and certainly by black belt, trainees ought to have some experience of this – otherwise the confidence which their ju-jitsu training should have instilled in them by then, may turn out to have hollow foundations.

Rehearsing in preparation for street violence is an important component of effective self-defence training. One way of achieving this is to put students in body armour and headguards (for safety) and let two attack one as if they were muggers. The defender can than give and take powerful blows which will give the student a much more realistic impression of what real violence implies.

Obviously, it is preferable not to get hit, but it is advisable to have some idea of what a physical attack actually feels like. Just how easy is it to prevent a strong, aggressive man grabbing you by the hair and punching you in the face? The other argument for this kind of training is the likelihood of surprise attacks; most muggers tend to attack from behind and normally work in gangs (or at least in twos), so that training exclusively with one-against-one does not prepare anyone for dealing with multiple assailants.

Leaving aside the physical aspects of self-defence for a moment, you should remember, if ever you find yourself in a situation where you are threatened with violence, the importance of the psychological aspect of combat. In Chapter 5 (when discussing blocking techniques) certain basic psychological concepts – relating to effective combat strategy – were mentioned. These included the idea of *sen* (first attack) *gonosen* (counter-attack) and the most difficult to grasp, *sen-no-sen*, (pre-emptive attack or beating the assailant to the punch). You will be much better prepared to defend yourself if you grasp and apply these concepts. There may be a moral dilemma for some but if you genuinely feel threatened by violence you are undoubtedly justified in acting first. The only thing you need for such justification is conviction.

Figs 139–44 Multiple attack (1). This first photograph of the sequence (Fig 139) shows tori grabbed over the arms from behind as a second assailant moves in to rob or strike him.

Fig 140 Tori immediately kicks the person facing him in the groin.

Fig 141 *Tori punches his right shoulder up and the left down, shrugging off his first attacker's grip, hitting him with a rear elbow strike to the ribs as he does so and grabbing his right wrist with his right hand.*

Fig 142 *Tori pulls his attacker's arm over his head and down into a shoulder-lock.*

Fig 143 *Maintaining the shoulder-lock, tori then grabs his hair.*

Fig 144 *He then pushes his first assailant on top of the other one, at which point he can disengage.*

115

WEAPONS TRAINING WITHIN JU-JITSU

Many modern ju-jitsu clubs train with traditional martial arts weapons, typically the indigenous Okinawan *nunchaku*, *sai*, *bo* and *jo*. Such training improves co-ordination and teaches the student effective *ma-ai* (distance evaluation) for dealing with armed attackers. Modern ju-jitsu exponents are also trained in methods for dealing with more modern weapons such as knives and guns. Ju-jitsu students do not, of course, train in the offensive use of such weapons in the dojo. Such training is or should be the sole province of soldiers, professional security guards and body-guards. In the United Kingdom only the police and the military are allowed to carry firearms; security guards and similar professions are only permitted to carry batons for defensive purposes. This is very much the exception on the world stage; in America private security companies, detectives, bounty-hunters and bodyguards are all licensed to carry fire-arms and the same is true in many European countries, notably Spain and Italy.

Key considerations in weapons training are the increased range which a particular weapon may give an attacker and the type of injury it is capable of inflicting. With the obvious exceptions of explosives and military hardware, projectile weapons are the most difficult with which to deal, firearms in particular, but there are a whole range of other more readily available implements, some of which are designed as weapons and others that can be used as weapons on the spur of the moment. Most of these other weapons are used either to bludgeon (clubs, bats, sticks, truncheons and so forth) or to cut (knives, razors, broken glass and so forth).

The type of weapon will probably give a good indication of how it will be used. The knife is possibly the most popular weapon of the mugger, 'street thug' or hooligan, but it is by no means the only one. The broken beer glass or bottle, knuckledusters, clubs, baseball bats, even ammonia sprays, figure prominently in street attacks. Modern ju-jitsu exponents train in a wide variety of techniques for dealing with any conceivable form of attack. The techniques which can be employed are virtually limitless, but should always be relevant to the nature of contemporary violence. It is beyond the scope of any single book on ju-jitsu to present the entire range of possible techniques, but it is important to consider two major areas of weapon defence which, incidentally, also help to indicate the adaptability of ju-jitsu.

Knife Defence

When threatened with a knife it is very important *not* to panic. You should aim to identify the type of weapon and how your attacker is holding it. Is it a slashing weapon or a stabbing weapon? Is it in his left or right hand? Is there anything lying around that you might be able to use as a weapon yourself, such as a brick, a bottle or a piece of wood? (Perhaps you can make him back off if there is.) If not, you should remain as calm and inoffensive as possible all the time, keep him talking and try to manoeuvre to a position which reduces the advantage his weapon gives him. As much as is feasible, keep just out of his striking range. Do not show fear, unless you want to lull him into a false sense of having the situation under control. Again, make no attempt to disarm him unless you have no choice; disarming an attacker of his knife must be a policy of last resort. If he wants money, perhaps

Fig 145–52 Knife defence (2). Initially (Fig 145) tori takes up a left free fighting stance as uke threatens a knife thrust to the stomach.

Fig 146 Tori sways out of the line of the attack and blocks uke's knife hand with a gedan-barai (downward block).

Fig 147 Tori follows up by initiating a reverse knife hand with a straight armlock.

Fig 148 Having struck with the knife hand to the side of the neck, tori pulls uke's hand down and brings him off balance.

117

Fig 149   Tori slams a hiza-geri (knee strike) into uke's solar plexus, maintaining his control of uke's right arm throughout the action.

Fig 150   Tori twists uke's arm through in a shoulder-lock, keeping his head down and keeping him in an awkward bent-over position.

Fig 151   If necessary, tori can transfer his right hand to uke's right hand and apply a hammer-lock in order to force uke to drop the knife, or to take it from him.

Fig 152   Tori takes the knife and keeps uke under control with a wrist- and shoulder-lock.

Fig 153–63   Knife defence (3). In this illustration (Fig 153) tori is standing normally and uke is threatening him with a knife.

Fig 154   Just as uke is about to use the knife tori pre-empts him by grabbing his wrist. . .

Fig 155   . . . simultaneously hitting him in the face with an elbow strike.

Fig 156   The elbow strike (opposite view).

Fig 157   Tori then immediately pushes the knife hand back and up and away from him, causing uke to bend forwards.

Fig 158   Tori reaches over uke's shoulder and, controlling uke's elbow with his chest, applies a reverse ude-garami, all the time pushing the knife up and away from him.

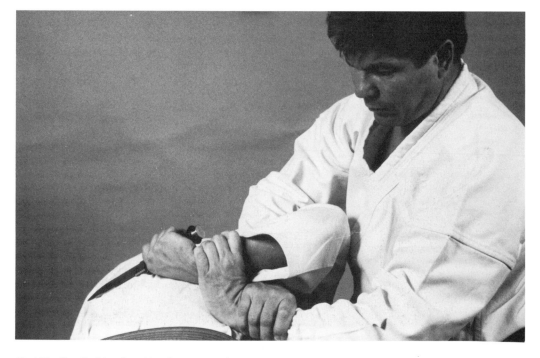

Fig 159   Detail of hand position for reverse ude-garami.

Fig 160 *Tori uses a* hiza-geri *(knee strike) to the pit of the stomach, which makes uke double up in pain.*

Fig 161 *Tori then levers up on uke's shoulder using the* ude-garami *to push him forwards and off balance. He simultaneously steps across with* sasae-tsuri-komi-ashi *to block uke's left foot and then throws him on his face.*

Fig 162 *Once uke is face down and helpless, tori applies the armlock to force him to drop the knife.*

Fig 163   Tori could then apply a double armlock if he wished to restrain his attacker without further injuring him.

Figs 164–70   Knife defence (4). Here (Fig 164) uke takes up a position to stab tori.

Fig 165   Tori side-steps uke's lunge and makes a knife-hand block.

Fig 166 He grabs uke's **arm** at the wrist and steps into him, delivering an elbow strike to the jaw.

Fig 167 Tori turns his back completely on uke and loops his right arm around uke's upper arm and grabs his own lapel. Note that the cutting edge of tori's right wrist is applied to the insertion of the triceps at the base of the elbow. Tori levers down on the wrist to apply a straight armlock, forcing uke to drop the knife.

Fig 168 Tori bends at the waist and rotates.

Fig 169 Tori throws uke to the ground with a maki-komi action, still in the armlock, and lands on his ribs.

Fig 170   Tori then releases his left hand, turns to his left and delivers a reverse elbow strike to uke's testicles.

Fig 171–4   Knife defence (5). In the first photograph of the sequence (Fig 171) uke attempts to stab at tori's throat.

Fig 172   Tori side-steps, catching uke's right wrist in his right hand and hits him immediately on the neck with a ridge-hand strike.

124

Fig 173 Trapping uke's knife hand in a bent wrist-lock, tori reaches around his neck with his left hand and takes his opposite collar. Tori then pulls uke off balance to his rear with the combined wrist-lock and strangulation effect.

Fig 174 Tori can pull uke to the floor and further consolidate his position by trapping uke's other arm with a leg entanglement. The strangle, applied correctly, will render uke unconscious in a matter of seconds.

you should comply; you have to calculate whether it is worth the risk of refusing his demand. At least if you decide to give him your money he will have his attention (and his hands) occupied with your wallet or purse. Is there any other way that you can distract him or set him up? When you have weighed all the variables, it is up to you to decide how to act. Every situation is unique; there are no hard-and-fast rules, only appropriate and inappropriate courses of action.

Gun Defences

Everything written regarding knife defence is even more relevant when dealing with guns. The gun is, without doubt, the weapon (prior to the development of the atom bomb) which most transformed the nature of warfare. In countries such as America it has also transformed everyday life in many parts of society. The prevalence of freely available firearms, particularly hand-guns, has led to soaring crime-rates and instances of life-threatening violence occurring ever more frequently. At a time when Beirut is constantly in the news as a result of interminable internecine urban warfare, you nevertheless run a greater risk, statistically speaking, of being shot walking down the street in Los Angeles. Most of the major cities in America, notably New York, Chicago, Detroit and Los Angeles are plagued by violent street crime and shootings are

125

Fig 175–9   Gun defence (1). In this photograph uke is holding a gun in his right hand and pointing it at tori's head. Tori is standing with his hands raised.

Fig 176   In a flash, tori makes his move, bringing both hands into play in a scissoring, clapping movement, but instead of clapping his hands he strikes the gun with his left hand and just below uke's wrist with his right.

Fig 177   Detail of the hand action shown in the previous photograph.

126

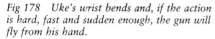

Fig 178 Uke's wrist bends and, if the action is hard, fast and sudden enough, the gun will fly from his hand.

Fig 179 Tori immediately follows up with a kick to the testicles.

commonplace. Nowhere is exempt from the danger; Washington DC is known as the murder capital of the United States. England, of course, is not America, but there is a thesis which asserts that everything that happens there sooner or later happens here. Certainly the influence of American culture, particularly through the cinema (and more recently through video) is enormous and other English speaking countries like Australia and Canada are being affected in a similar way.

Perhaps very obvious, but worth saying nonetheless is that the great problem with guns is the ease with which it becomes possible for one person to kill another. No special intelligence or training is required, the shooter simply has to aim and pull the trigger, and at the time of writing if you are to find yourself threatened with a gun in the United Kingdom, the chances are it would probably be

youngsters with air weapons rather than real firearms. Among more 'serious' criminals, such as bank robbers, hand-guns and sawn-off shotguns are preferred weapons for armed robbery, but thankfully the use of such weapons has not yet filtered through to the mugger. In these days of international travel, however, it is naive to assume that other countries' criminals are as restrained by the law and by the below average availability of firearms in the United Kingdom. Neglecting to practise gun defence because it seems unlikely ever to be relevant to your daily life is like not fastening your seat belt in your car because you do not think you will have a crash: simply shortsighted.

One point to be remembered with gun defences is that they are designed to deal with the *threat* of a gun. They are considerably more useful and practicable when someone is using the gun to coerce you

Fig 180–8 Gun defence (2). Fig 180 shows uke pointing a gun at tori's chest. Tori has his hands raised.

Fig 181 With a slight tai-sabaki *tori quickly grabs uke's hand and, pressing his thumbs against the gun, twists it away from him so that it points instead at uke.*

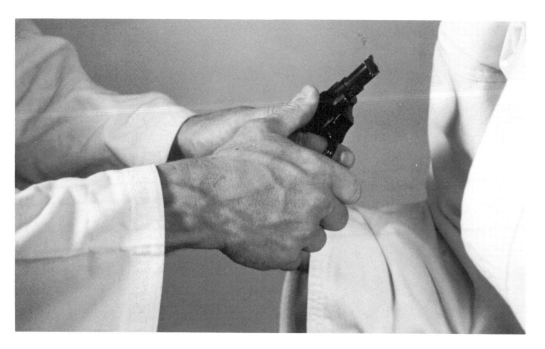

Fig 182   *This shows the detail of the grip. It should be used against a man holding the gun in his right hand.*

Fig 183   *The technique feels as though you are grabbing quickly, as if you were trying to catch a mosquito, and of then pushing to the right, making a small circle and changing the direction forwards and in towards uke. The initial direction is, of course, reversed against a left-handed man.*

Fig 184 With uke's wrist painfully locked up, tori continues the direction of the twist anticlockwise.

Fig 185 Stepping forward on his right foot and turning to his left, tori forces uke so far off balance that he is forced to fall to avoid breaking his wrist.

Fig 186 This shows the detail of the grip: using the gun as a lever, thumb, fingers and wrist are all controlled.

Fig 187 Once on the ground, tori can easily take the gun from uke.

Fig 188 Tori then delivers a stamp-kick to the jaw to knock uke unconscious. Note that throughout the technique the barrel of the gun is never pointing at tori and if uke does pull the trigger at any stage he is likely to shoot himself.

Figs 189–95 Gun defence (3). As in the previous sequences, uke is threatening tori with a gun. Here (Fig 189) uke is pointing a pistol at tori's chest.

Fig 190 Tori quickly catches the gun in both hands fingers on top, thumbs under the trigger guard, and he immediately twists the weapon so that it is pointing upwards.

131

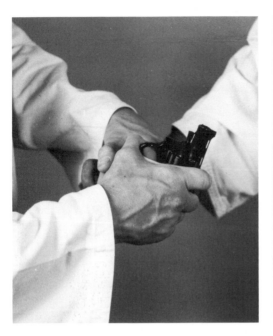

Fig 191   This shows the detail of the grip: it locks uke's wrist and also the trigger-guard puts his finger in a lock. Applied with a snap this technique will break the gunman's finger.

Fig 192   The gun hand is twisted inwards so that it is pointing at uke. The twisting action of the hands is similar to the wrist action when casting with a fishing line.

Fig 193   Tori then steps away and blocks uke's straight arm at the elbow with hara-gatame, forcing him face down on the ground.

Fig 194   Tori then disarms uke.

Fig 195   Note the use of the trigger-guard to maintain a finger lock.

into handing over your money, to menace and to threaten you than for defending yourself if someone with a gun is intent upon killing you. Whether you choose to defend yourself against a gunman is entirely your own decision and will probably depend upon the nature of the crime being committed and the feasibility of making the chosen technique work. Such a decision is never easy. Policemen in countries such as America face such situations almost routinely but do have the advantage of being armed themselves. With both gun and knife defence techniques it is vitally important to practise on both sides, left and right. The simpler the technique, the more important it is to practise.

GROUND TECHNIQUES

The fact that an assailant has been knocked down, thrown or otherwise brought to the ground does not mean that the danger has passed. In some cases a single blow may render an assailant unconscious but in others it may only wind or stun your attacker; you should always remember that if he is still conscious he is still dangerous. Although it is generally not a good idea to fight the assailant on the ground when defending yourself (because of the danger from accomplices) ju-jitsu is a complete fighting system and in a one-against-one confrontation provides a variety of methods for finishing off an attacker.

Following up after a throw can involve techniques as varied as knee-drops, stamping kicks, strangleholds and joint-locks. The follow-up is determined by the circumstances, the severity of the initial attack and the potential future threat the individual represents.

In keeping with the original tenets of Japanese *budo*, ju-jitsu training also covers responses to situations where attack may seem unlikely. The *samurai* were trained to be on the alert constantly for the unexpected attack and ever ready to respond to danger. *Samurai* paranoia (or far-sightedness) extended to anticipating treachery and surprise attack even at the dinner table and in the bath. The legendary Miyamoto Musashi, the author of the classic treatise on strategy, *Go Rin no Sho*, (*A Book of Five Rings*) was reputed to have refrained from bathing for a number of years to avoid the risk of making himself vulnerable to his numerous enemies. Such precautions are, needless to say, excessive but it is as well to know how to respond in an everyday situation that suddenly becomes dangerous. Ju-jitsu students practise a number of defences from standing, seated and prone positions in an effort to cover every eventuality.

One further matter to bear in mind is that you may not necessarily only be attacked in a city where the ground is hard and dry. It is equally possible that you could be attacked while sitting in the car, lying on a beach or walking in a slippery, muddy field. In fact many fighting systems have been strongly influenced by geographical conditions. *Pentjak silat*, an Indonesian fighting art, was devised for fighting in mountainous yet muddy terrain where it was almost impossible to retain one's footing during the rainy season. As a result a highly elaborate system of ground fighting was developed.

Ground defences are essentially emergency techniques that can be employed when you are knocked down, slip or are attacked while lying down or seated. Ju-jitsu ground techniques are more easily applied than those in judo even though the end result may be identical; this is

Fig 196–8 Ground defences (1). Here (Fig 196) uke is on top of tori, between his legs, and is attempting to strangle him.

Fig 197   Tori grabs uke's wrists and immediately throws his legs over uke's shoulders, crossing his feet behind his head.

Fig 198 (left)   Tori raises his hips and pulls uke's arms straight, pushing against uke's elbow to apply a double armlock. This is a very powerful technique but requires great training if a woman is to use it effectively against a heavier, stronger man.

Figs 199–203   Ground defences (2). This photograph (Fig 199) shows uke on top of tori, attempting to strangle him.

Fig 200   Tori puts his right foot inside uke's left leg and reaching straight up with his left hand, he grabs hold of uke's left elbow.

Fig 201 (left) Using the power of his legs, tori pushes uke's left hand off his neck and grabs uke's arm at the elbow with his own left hand.

Fig 202 Tori then rolls to his left by using his right leg and left arm grip in order to flick uke over on to his back.

137

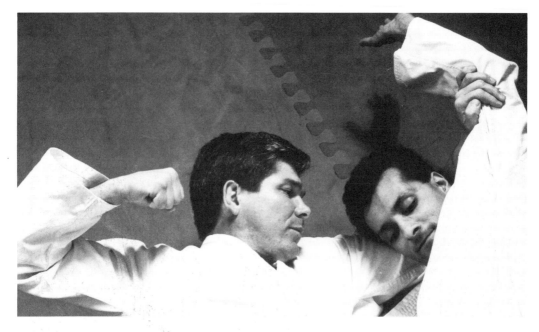

Fig 203   Tori rolls on top of uke's right arm and, keeping his left arm trapped, can follow up with a punch to the face.

Fig 204–9   Sangaku-waza (triangle techniques) can be very effective for ground fighting. Fig 204 shows the basic sangaku-jime: from the between-the-legs position tori swivels and throws his leg across uke's neck, pulling uke's head down to prevent him escaping.

Fig 205   Tori grabs uke's wrist with his right hand.

Fig 206   Tori throws his left leg over his right, so that the instep of the right foot
fits in snugly behind the left knee. To apply the strangle, tori squeezes with his legs.

Fig 207   In the same position an armlock is also possible if tori grabs uke's wrist
with both hands and levers him up with the hips.

Fig 208   Tori can, if he wishes, twist his hips to the side and go for a double
armlock.

140

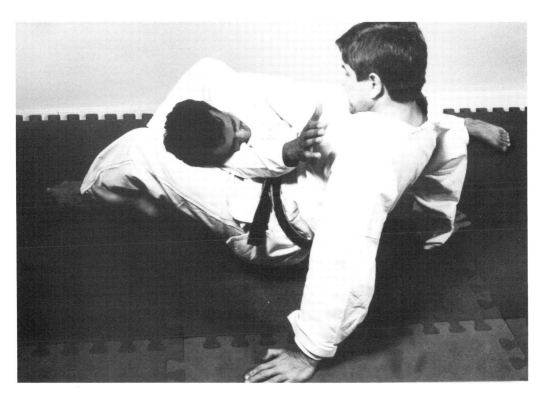

Fig 209   *If tori wants to render uke unconscious, but finds him to be exceptionally strong, tori should support himself on his hands and raise his hips off the ground. This means his full weight is added to the squeezing effect on uke's neck.*

because it is permitted to use *atemi-waza* to soften up an assailant. In essence the techniques are often the same. There are obvious dangers inherent in adopting some ground fighting positions, but for the most part these positions are transitory and the risk taken is no greater than in applying any other technique. One important tip is always to keep the testicles protected; remember that this is perhaps the most vulnerable part of the male anatomy.

Ground fighting is an important aspect of ju-jitsu, not least because it can be the last line of defence for women when fighting off rapists. Accordingly its study is especially recommended for women students concerned to ensure their safety. Although weight and strength become

more important when fighting on the ground – and the woman may be at a disadvantage in terms of physical size and power – there are some extremely effective groundwork techniques that can incapacitate even the strongest attacker.

Fitness

To employ a ju-jitsu technique successfully when defending yourself does not necessarily require great strength or fitness. Timing, skill, speed and confidence are the crucial factors in such situations. However, being fit should be a natural result of ju-jitsu training and is never a disadvantage since physical fitness is very important both for daily life and for getting through long, hard training sessions. The fitter you are, the more effectively you can improve your skills and, in all probability, the healthier you will be. Callisthenics play a part in almost all ju-jitsu training sessions, serving to warm up trainees for the actual practice of ju-jitsu and simultaneously improving stamina, strength and flexibility. These elements (flexibility, speed, strength, stamina and skill) can improve by regular training.

The ju-jitsu exponent worried about fitness is advised to run two or three times a week for half an hour or so, preferably in the early morning, and ought to practise sprinting for explosive speed and power once a week. Heavier people may find swimming a suitable alternative to running (which can cause joint problems, particularly when the running surface is hard). Once basic good physical condition is achieved training becomes much less arduous and more productive since it is easier to concentrate on technical aspects when you have your breathing under control.

10 Traditional Ju-jitsu: the Roots of the Art

The student wishing to understand fully the extent of the differences between the classical and modern systems of ju-jitsu is recommended to study the *koshiki-no-kata*, the *kime-no-kata* and the more modern *go-shin-jutsu-no-kata*. The first of these, *koshiki-no-kata*, illustrates how to deal with an armoured foe and is a fascinating study in itself, but is very neglected because modern students tend not to see its relevance. This a great pity as some remarkable insights can be gained by practising it. These *kata*, which embody the traditional wisdom of ju-jitsu, are the essence of the art.

CLASSICAL JU-JITSU

The *kime-no-kata* (forms of self-defence) is also known as the *shinken-shobu-no-kata* (forms of combat). *Shinken shobu* means a fight to the finish. The *kata* comprises the demonstration of self-defence techniques against a variety of unarmed and armed attacks and dates back to the fifteenth century. The *kata* consists of twenty sequences of techniques and is divided into two groups, the first of which comprises eight defences against attacks in the seated posture. The *kata* also includes grabbing, striking, knife and sword defences. The first section is known as *idori* and the techniques it contains date back to the time when Japanese houses contained no chairs and much of daily life, from eating a meal to doing business, involved sitting cross-legged or kneeling on mats.

The second group of techniques is called *tachi-ai*, (standing defences) and the majority of the techniques it contains remain as relevant today as they ever were, although the likelihood of being attacked with a sword is admittedly less likely than it once was.

Kime-no-kata

Seated defences (*idori*)

Ryote-dori	two-handed wrist grab
Tsukkake	punch to the stomach
Suri-age	palm-heel strike to the face
Yoko-uchi	hammer-fist to the temple
Ushiro-dori	overarm grasp from behind
Tsukkomi	stabbing thrust to the stomach
Kiri-komi	slashing attack to the face
Yoko-tsuki	stabbing thrust from the side

Standing defences (*tachi-ai*)

Ryote-dori	two-handed wrist grab
Sode-tori	sleeve grab
Tsukkake	punch to face
Tsuki-age	upper-cut
Suri-age	palm-heel strike
Yoko-uchi	punch from the side

Ke-age	kick to the groin
Ushiro-dori	two-handed grab from the rear
Tsukkomi	stab thrust to the stomach
Kiri-komi	slash to the face
Nuki-kake	blocking the sword-drawing attack
Kiri-oroshi	downward cut with sword

Description of the Kata: Idori

For the sake of convenience, it is assumed in the following sections that both tori and uke are male. The *kime-no-kata* is a highly formalised series of movements performed in accordance with an elaborate and established ritual. It begins with both exponents facing each other approximately twelve feet apart, tori to the right of *joseki* (small shrine), uke to the left. Uke holds a *katana* (sword) and a *tanto* (dagger) in his right hand at belt level, hilts uppermost. Both participants pivot slightly and bow to the *joseki* and then resume their positions facing one another. They then both simultaneously kneel in *seiza* (basic kneeling posture), first dropping the left knee to the ground on the level of the right heel and then the right with the toes bent and extended back along the mat. Initially the knees are bent at forty-five degrees and the hips are kept high for a moment (as in praying) before both participants then sit back on their heels into *seiza*. Uke then places the sword and dagger to the right of his right hip, the sword on the outside and the dagger close to his right leg, parallel to the axis of the *kata*. The hilts of both weapons must be to the front and the edges facing towards uke.

Uke then stands up, turns his back on tori and withdraws about nine feet from the axis of the *kata* to the point where he arrived on the mat, kneels, his back turned to tori, and slowly lowers his weapons to the mat, points first, the edges kept towards him, the hilts pointing to *joseki*. Uke then rises and returns to face tori who rises at the same time so that they meet in the middle of the mat.

They again kneel and approach each other on their knees and with clenched fists until their knees are about six inches apart. At this distance they bow to one another, both leaning slightly to the right in order not to bang their heads. They remain kneeling for a few seconds, face to face, in *taiza*, breathing deeply and concentrating to get into the mood of the *kata*. This position, in which their knees are the breadth of two hands apart, is called *hiza-zume*.

Kneeling opposite one another the participants perform the first technique of the *kata: ryote-dori*, the two-handed grab. Uke sits up and grabs both tori's wrists with an orthodox grip, thumbs inside, fingers outside. Tori reacts by putting his weight on his left knee and raising and separating his hands at the same time. This movement causes uke to fall forwards, whereupon tori delivers an *atemi* strike, kicking uke in the solar plexus with the ball of his right foot, making a *kiai* shout as the kick reaches its target. Tori then puts his right knee back on the ground and takes an encircling grip on uke's wrist with both hands. Tori then rotates on his right knee, raising the other knee and stepping on his left foot as uke's arm is pulled across his upper chest, trapping his extended elbow under his armpit. Uke applies pressure on the trapped elbow with *waki-gatame* and tori taps the mat twice to indicate submission.

Tori and uke resume the *hiza-zume* position for the second technique, *tsukkake,* this time about a foot apart from each other. Uke sits up, raising his toes, and aims a punch at tori's solar plexus making a *kiai* as he does so. Tori evades the blow by pivoting a quarter turn to the right and raising his right knee, simultaneously grabs uke's right wrist with the left hand and pulls uke forwards off balance in the direction of the blow and on to an *atemi* strike with the right hand between the eyes to the base of nose. Note that both punches are made with the palm kept uppermost. The wrist grab and punch must be perfectly synchronised to demonstrate how uke's initial attack is used to tori's advantage and how the pull combines with push.

Tori then grabs uke's right hand with his own right hand, palm facing downwards and pulls it across his body until the forearm is resting against his thigh and the elbow pulled tight against his abdomen! Tori then reaches around uke's neck with his left hand, grabbing uke's right lapel in a looping choke. Uke is forced to submit by applying *hara-gatame* in conjunction with the choke. Uke indicates submission by tapping the mat twice.

Both exponents return to *hiza-zume*. Uke attacks with the third technique, *suri-age*, raising his hips and coming up on his toes, attempting to make a palm-heel strike to the base of tori's nose or the forehead, with the intention of driving tori's head back. Tori, too, raises his hips and toes, but sways his head back out of range and immediately brings up both hands, the right deflecting the blow upwards and grabbing uke's right wrist (tori's hand is palm-up with fingers uppermost and thumb underneath). Tori places his left hand on uke's shoulder and takes the weight on his left knee, delivering a kick to the solar plexus with his right foot. He then pivots to the right on his left knee as he brings the right knee down and

uses both hands to pull uke forwards and off balance, driving him face down into the mat. Tori elicits a submission by kneeling on the back of uke's arm just above the elbow joint and pulling up with his right hand. Both men return to *hiza-zume*.

The fourth technique is *yoko-uchi*. Uke launches an attack with this technique; a hooking roundhouse swing aimed at tori's temple. Uke kneels up and pulls back his right arm in preparation to deliver the blow. He attacks with a *kiai* shout and tori immediately raises his right knee and ducks to his left under the blow, wrapping his right arm across uke's chest and over his neck. Tori simultaneously ducks under the blow and pushes the side of his head into the back of uke's shoulder, catching uke's right hip at the back with his left hand and pushing him on to his back. Landing almost in *kata-gatame* tori immediately raises his upper body, presses against the back of uke's right elbow, lifts his right elbow high with the fingers of his right hand open and delivers a downwards elbow strike to the base of the sternum. Both men then kneel about four feet apart.

For the fifth technique, *ushiro-dori* (hold from the rear), uke stands and walks around behind tori, passing on his right side. He then seats himself in a kneeling posture some eight inches behind tori. He supports himself on his left knee and steps with his right foot to the side of tori's right knee, shouting as he does so and grabbing tori in an overarm grasp around his upper arms and body. Tori reacts by immediately raising his arms and sliding his right leg back between uke's legs, rising on to his toes as he does so. At the same time he grabs as high on uke's left sleeve with his left hand as he can reach and traps his left hand to his chest using his right hand. He then smoothly rolls uke over his left shoulder in a *seoi-nage* action. As the throw is completed tori continues the rotation of his upper body to end up in a position similar to *ushiro-kesa-gatame*. He controls uke's hips with his right hand and delivers an *atemi* fore-fist strike to the testicles with his left hand. Both partners then assume the position from which they began this technique.

Once tori has resumed his normal starting position, uke gets up and walks back, and then around and in front on tori's right side, performing a kneeling bow before getting up to go and fetch his dagger. Kneeling in front of the weapons he picks up the dagger and places it blade up inside his jacket over the left hip and above his belt, concealing it with his *gi*. Uke then returns to *hiza-zume*, kneeling about twenty inches in front of tori.

The sixth technique, *tsukkomi*, is a dagger thrust to the stomach. Uke grips the scabbard through his *judogi* and draws the blade with his right hand. He raises his hips and steps forwards with his left foot while making a *kiai* shout, thrusts the *tanjo* at tori's solar plexus. Tori pivots to his right on his left knee, stepping up with his right and deflects the thrust with his left hand, grabbing uke's right wrist and pulling him on to an *atemi* fore-fist strike to the bridge of the nose with his

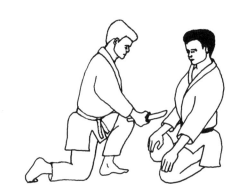

Fig 211

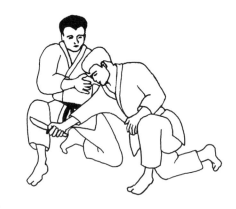

Fig 212

Figs 210–13 Tsukkomi; *dagger thrust to the stomach.*

Fig 213

146

right hand. Tori makes a *kiai* as he strikes and then grabs uke's right wrist with his right hand and pulls his arm into his stomach as he reaches over with his left hand to grab uke's left lapel. He then simultaneously applies a choke and *hara-gatame* exactly as in the second technique and uke submits. Both men resume *hiza-zume* and uke replaces the dagger in its scabbard.

The seventh technique, *kiri-komi* is a downward slash to tori's head using the cutting edge of the dagger. Uke reaches inside his jacket with his right hand and takes out the sheathed weapon. He takes the dagger from its sheath with his left thumb and draws it with his right hand. In one movement he raises his hips and steps up on his right foot as he lifts the dagger above his head to bring it down in a cutting slash at tori's face. As he attacks he makes a *kiai* shout. Tori pivots on his left knee and comes up on his right foot, catching uke's wrist with his right hand underneath and his left hand on top. Tori rotates to his right pulling uke's arm straight and unbalancing him; he then traps his elbow under his armpit, focusing his weight there. He applies *waki-gatame* by twisting further to the right, forcing uke to submit. Uke then returns to his original position, resheaths the dagger and puts it back in his jacket on the left side.

The last technique in the *idori* group is *yoko-tsuki*, a dagger thrust from the side. Uke stands, walks over to tori's right side and kneels about eight inches to his right, facing in the same direction. Once again gripping the scabbard through his jacket, uke draws the weapon with his right hand. Stepping towards tori on his left foot he tries to stab him in the side. Tori, however, comes up on the toes of his left foot and pivots 180 degrees to the right on his left knee, raising his right knee as he does so.

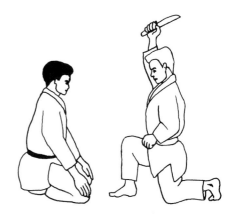

Figs 214–16   Kiri-komi; *dagger slash at the head.*

Fig 215

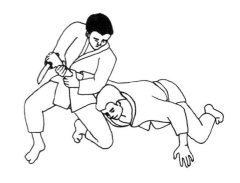

Fig 216

147

Tori deflects the knife arm at the elbow with the palm of the left hand and immediately strikes uke between the eyes. Tori immediately transfers his right hand to uke's right wrist and pulls it into his right hip to apply *hara-gatame*, simultaneously looping his left arm around uke's neck to apply a choke. Uke is forced to submit.

Uke returns to kneel facing tori about three feet away, then places the dagger back in his jacket, stands and turns around to walk to where the sword is. He kneels and lays the dagger down in its original position. This concludes the *idori* section of the *kata*.

Figs 217–19 Ryote-dori; *two-handed grab.*

Fig 218

Description of the Kata: Tachi-ai

Ryote-dori (two-handed grab); both men rise to commence the *tachi-ai* whereupon uke turns and walks to about three feet away from tori, pausing there for a second. He then shouts and steps forward with his right foot to grab both tori's wrists. Tori steps back and pulls up and out with his arms, breaking uke's balance. Tori simultaneously kicks uke in the testicles with the ball of his right foot. Tori immediately puts his right foot back on the ground and steps back and to his left with his left foot, gripping uke's left wrist from underneath with his right hand, pulling the left hand free as he does so. He then straightens uke's arm, trapping his elbow under his armpit and applying *waki-gatame* with the knees well bent.

Sode-tori (sleeve grab); uke walks behind tori, passing on his right side, and positions himself to his left rear corner. Uke grabs the middle of tori's left sleeve with his left hand before grabbing it with his right and releasing it with his left. Uke twists and pushes tori's arm to force him to walk forwards. Tori makes two steps

Fig 219

with his right then his left foot. On the third step he steps diagonally forwards and to his right, unbalancing uke in that direction, and makes a stamping side-kick to uke's knee with the side of his left foot. Tori immediately puts his left foot down, pivots through 180 degrees to his left and grabs uke by the right sleeve with his left hand and the left lapel with his right hand; he then brings uke down by 'reaping away' his right leg with right *o-soto-gari*.

Tsukkake (punch to the face); both men stand about eight feet apart. Uke makes a long step on his left foot and lifts his left fist to head height, holding his right fist at stomach height ready to deliver a punch. Uke then steps forward quickly on his right foot, making a lunge punch attack with his right fist. Tori quickly steps in front of him and to his left (on his left foot), then turning to his right to avoid the blow. He catches uke's right forearm with his right hand, grips the top of the arm, and pulls him forwards and down, breaking his balance to the front.

Figs 220–3   Sode-tori; *grip on the sleeve.*

Fig 221

Fig 222

Fig 223

Fig 224–7   Tusakkake; *punch to the face.*

Fig 225

Fig 226

Fig 227

Tori quickly steps behind him, stepping first with his right foot then his left, then slipping his right arm around uke's neck from the front as he steps. As uke attempts to recover his balance and straighten up tori applies *hadaka-jime* (the naked strangle), clasping his hands and jamming the side of his head into the back of uke's head. Tori steps well back with his left foot to cause uke to arch backwards into a very weak position and then consolidates the choke.

Tsuki-age (upper-cut); for this technique tori and uke begin about three feet apart. Uke steps forwards on his right foot, shouts and attempts to hit tori with a right upper-cut to the chin. Tori sways his head out of range and catches uke's wrist with both hands, pulling it upwards in the direction in which it is already moving. Tori then makes a corkscrew motion with the upper body and rotates to his right, pulling uke's elbow under his left armpit and then applies *waki-gatame*.

Suri-age (palm-heel strike to forehead); tori and uke stand about three feet apart. Uke steps forwards on his right foot and launches a palm-heel strike at tori's forehead, shouting as he does so. Tori bends his knees and lifts his left hand to block the blow at uke's elbow with his forearm. Having parried the attack, tori immediately counters with a punch to the solar plexus, making a *kiai* as he does so. He then quickly steps into uke on his left foot and slides his left arm around uke's upper back, placing the palm of the hand on his lower back and catching the left sleeve with his right hand. Tori completes the technique by bringing his right foot back and flipping uke over his hip with *uki-goshi*.

Yoko-uchi (hammer-fist to the temple); tori and uke begin this sequence about three feet apart with uke stepping forwards on his left foot and lifting his right fist above his head. He uses his forward momentum to swing a downwards, oblique punch at tori's right temple, stepping forwards on his right foot as he completes the blow. Tori side-steps to the left and ducks, stepping diagonally to his left to position himself to uke's right. He simultaneously slips his right arm under uke's right armpit and reaches across his chest to grab his left lapel, his thumb touching uke's collar-bone. Tori quickly steps behind uke and reaches around his neck from behind with his left hand and grabs deep inside uke's collar, just below the ear. The hand position is that used for *okuri-eri-jime*, the sliding lapel strangle, and tori applies the technique by stepping back on his left foot to bend uke backwards off balance and by digging his forehead in the nape of uke's neck.

Ke-age (kick to the groin); tori and uke resume their starting positions three feet apart. Uke makes a small step forwards

on his left foot and launches a kick with his right foot at tori's groin. Tori steps back on his right foot and pivots on his left, avoiding the kick. Tori quickly catches uke's heel from underneath with his left hand and then places his right hand on the ankle and pushes the leg to the left. Twisting his hips to the left, tori utters a *kiai* and kicks uke in the groin with his right foot.

Ushiro-dori (rear hold); both men resume their starting position three feet apart and uke then proceeds to walk around behind tori, passing on his right side to take up his position two and a half feet behind him. Both men then take a step forward with the left foot, whereupon uke makes a step on his right foot and grabs tori around the upper arms. Tori immediately lifts his elbows upwards and outwards and grabs uke's right sleeve with both hands. Tori slides his right leg back and between uke's legs, drops underneath and throws him with *ippon-seoi-otoshi*, his right knee touching the floor as the throw is completed. Tori follows up with a knife-hand strike to the bridge of uke's nose and a *kiai*. Both men then stand up and, as in the *idori* set, uke goes to get the dagger and then returns to stand facing tori, about three feet away.

Tsukkomi (stab thrust to the stomach); uke grips the scabbard through his jacket with his left hand and draws the dagger with his right. He steps forward on his left foot shouting and attempting to stab tori in the stomach. Tori steps back on his right foot, deflecting the thrust with his left hand and immediately punching uke between the eyes (while making a *kiai* shout). Tori instantly grabs uke's right wrist with his right hand and pulls it in to his right hip, trapping the forearm against his thigh. Tori then reaches around uke's neck and grabs his lapel with his left

151

Figs 228–32   Ushiro-dori; *grab from behind.*

Fig 229

Fig 230

Fig 231

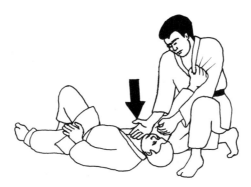

Fig 232

Fig 223–6   Nuki-kake; *blocking sword draw.*

Fig 234

Fig 235

Fig 236

hand. He steps forward on his right foot and then again on his left, pulling uke's arm straight across his abdomen, applying a choke simultaneously with *hara-gatame*.

Kiri-komi (slash to the face); tori and uke face each other three feet apart. Uke takes the dagger from his jacket with his right hand and sticks it in his belt on his left side. He then stands in *shizentai* again. He frees the dagger with his left thumb and draws it with his right hand, lifting it overhead. He shouts and steps forwards on his right foot trying to slash at the top of tori's head. Tori sways just out of range and reaches up to catch uke's wrist with both hands. Tori then steps back on his right foot and turns to the left. Tori steps with his left foot just in front of uke's right and, levering down with his bent elbow against uke's straight arm, traps him in *waki-gatame*.

Uke and tori resume their positions facing one another and uke resheaths the dagger. He then takes it out of his belt

153

and puts it back in his jacket. He turns and goes over to the sword, where he replaces the dagger in its original position and picks up the sword. He places the sword in his belt on the left side with the cutting edge uppermost and returns to face tori, stopping about five feet away from him.

Nuki-kake (blocking the sword-drawing attack); uke takes hold of the scabbard with his left hand and places his right on the handle. He steps forwards on his right foot and attempts to draw the sword. Tori anticipates his intention and steps in with his right foot close to uke's right foot and grabs his right wrist with his own right hand on top. Tori takes a large step to uke's rear with his right root, quickly bringing the left foot around behind him also. He turns so that he is behind uke and facing him and reaches around his neck with his left hand, grabbing high on his right lapel. He releases his grip on uke's wrist and lifts his right hand up and under uke's right armpit and behind his neck, putting him in a *kata-ha-jime* chokehold. Tori steps back to keep uke off balance and to apply the technique. Unable to use his hands, uke signals his surrender by stamping on the mat with his foot.

Kiri-oroshi (downward cut with the sword); tori and uke take their positions about eight feet apart. Uke steps forward with his right foot and slowly draws the sword. He holds the tip in the *seigen* position, level with tori's eyes. Uke advances with a *tsugi-ashi* step and tori takes a step back on his left foot. Uke then steps forward on his left foot and raises the sword to the *jodan* position, high above his head. Uke shouts and attacks, attempting to cut at the top of tori's head. Tori evades the blow by stepping to his left front corner and then turning to his right.

He quickly grabs uke's right wrist in both hands, fingers above, thumb underneath. Tori then pulls uke's right arm into his stomach, taking the hand past his thigh, forcing him down towards his right front corner. Tori reaches around his neck with his left hand holding high on the lapel and then applies a choke, stepping forward with his right foot and then his left. He takes one more step with his right foot and applies *hara-gatame*. Uke signifies his surrender by releasing his grip on the sword with his left hand to tap tori's leg. This is the final *kime-no-kata* technique.

Uke then stands at a point about six feet from tori and, holding the sword point down, takes a step back and brings the sword point up to eye level. He then resheaths the sword, takes another step back and stands naturally. Uke then returns to the dagger and lays the sword down next to it. He then picks up both sword and dagger in his right hand and returns to face tori. Both take a step backwards together, kneel and bow to each other, uke laying aside his weapons on his right before he does so. Uke picks up the sword and dagger in his right hand and both men stand, turn to face *joseki* and perform a standing bow.

The *kime-no-kata* can be performed as a training exercise in its own right in order to develop effective self-defence techniques, but many contemporary practitioners find the attention to etiquette onerous and it is only usually seen resurrected occasionally for demonstration purposes and sometimes for grading.

Even the most hardened modernist should be able to learn a great deal from this *kata*, however, and its study cannot be too highly recommended. The rhythm and patterns of the *kata* are very revealing and certain aspects are repeated as if to stress their importance. Every time uke attacks he shouts, but every time tori counter-attacks it is with a louder *kiai*. In most cases, before a locking technique is applied, an *atemi* strike to the region of the eyes or bridge of the nose is made, so performing an important distracting function. By implication the importance of *hara-* and *waki-gatame* as self-defence techniques (especially when weapons are involved) ought to be obvious.

Goshin jutsu

Where the *kime-no-kata* embodies the knowledge of the old ju-jitsu schools, the *goshin-jutsu kata* is the encapsulation of the modern self-defence ideas of the Kodokan's best minds. Devised in 1957 it comprises twenty-one techniques and is intended to complement the *kime-no-kata*.

Esoteric Aspects of Ju-jitsu

All of the martial arts have their esoteric or secret aspects and ju-jitsu is no exception. There is a tradition in ju-jitsu of developing the internal forces as well as the purely physical or muscular. This is supposedly achieved by developing the *shitahara*. *Hara* is the Japanese word for centre or stomach. The *saika tanden* is the spot corresponding to your centre of gravity. The *tanden* is the navel and the *saika tanden* is a spot about two inches below. Intrinsically linked to the idea of the centre and the *saika tanden* is the concept of *ki* (*chi* in Chinese) which is difficult to translate but which may be rendered as vital force of life energy.

There are many methods reputed to develop *ki* and in some forms of aikido, the physical aspects of training are said to be meaningless without it. One method of training to develop *ki* is as follows.

Sit in a meditation posture such as the half-lotus postion (this can be made easier for the beginner by sitting on a cushion). Tie your belt or a cloth sash one or two inches below your naval. Put a pebble between the belt and your lower abdomen – the pebble should be two inches directly below your navel. Inhale slowly, taking about five seconds to fill your lungs, and try to feel as though you are breathing the air down as far as the point where the pebble is pressing against you. Imagine it swelling with the air. When you have finished inhaling, hold your breath and contract the muscles of the lower abdomen. You should aim to feel as though the action of pulling your stomach muscles up and in is meeting with the inhaled air pushing down and out. It is very difficult to express this in words and, of course, the air is not actually doing what you are imagining, but the aim is to cultivate an awareness of a particular feeling. Hold this pressure for five seconds, then exhale, again taking about five seconds to empty your lungs and relaxing the sensation of internal abdominal pressure, but trying to retain an awareness of the sensation at the *tanden*. This should be repeated, paying particular attention to your breathing and concentrating on these new sensations, for ten minutes in the morning and again for ten minutes at night. If you feel breathless at any point, break off and breathe until your breathing returns to normal. This exercise requires at least three months' practice, repeated every day, if it is to have an effect.

One of the most interesting examples known to the author of *ki* being tested occurred when the well-known judo and ju-jitsu expert Brian Jacks – who has always had the typical healthy scepticism of the contest judoman for things esoteric – encountered a West German 8th dan in ki-jutsu at a martial arts demonstration. The German had given an impressive display of freeing himself from numerous of his students who had attempted unsuccessfully to immobilise him, when he threw out a challenge to anyone present. Brian Jacks took up the offer and applied *kesa-gatame*, the basic scarf hold from which the 8th dan could not escape. When asked to explain why the mysterious *ki* had failed to work against the Englishman he maintained that Brian Jacks had a very highly developed *ki* of his own, even though it was unconscious. An open mind is very important in the martial arts, but everyone must draw their own conclusions from what they themselves have experienced.

Afterword

JU-JITSU: THE FUTURE

Having read this far the differences between judo, aikido, karate and ju-jitsu should be as clear as the similarities between the various disciplines. The reader should also have a good understanding of the differences that exist between classical and modern schools of ju-jitsu.

At no stage have I attempted to 'systematise' or catalogue the techniques of ju-jitsu; such a task is beyond the scope of a single book. What has been attempted is to present the ancient and modern arts side by side with representative techniques and training methods from both traditions. It is to be hoped that students of other martial arts such as karate and judo will be able to learn much that may be useful to them in their own discipline.

The great value of ju-jitsu is not simply in its practical application for the purposes of self-defence; as a system it offers more than just battlefield techniques for defeating an enemy. The practice of modern ju-jitsu offers physical training alongside the cultivation of social attitudes and moral values. It is the great paradox of the martial arts that those who practise them achieve peace through the study of the arts of war and violence.

So far as the effectiveness of ju-jitsu techniques is concerned, the same is true

Fig 237   Mu-ga; *selflessness.*

of them as for all other martial arts; they are as effective as the person employing them is competent. Real competence takes many years of training and often the difference between an effective technique and one that fails may be only a very small point, but those small points can mean the difference between life and death.

157

Glossary

Aikido Japanese martial art founded by Morihei Ueshiba, literally meaning 'way of harmony'. It is characterised by use of throwing, locking and immobilising techniques as opposed to violent striking methods. Of all martial arts it has the highest ethical basis.
Aiki-jutsu A combat system based on the integrated use of energy or *ki* which served as the core curriculum for the 'generation of aikido'.
Ashi-waza Foot techniques, footsweep.
Ate-waza Techniques used for striking an attacker's joints.
Atemi-waza Striking techniques aimed at vital points of the body.

Bo Japanese quarterstaff.
Bo-jutsu Techniques using the staff.
Bugei Classical martial combative systems; bu-jutsu.
Bushi A warrior or fighting man.
Bushido The way of the warrior; the moral code and belief system of Japan's *samurai*.

Dan Grade indicating level of proficiency in Japanese culture.

Hara The pit of the stomach; there is a Japanese belief that the centre of a person's being is to be found in the *hara*.

Iai-do Classical art of sword drawing and re-sheathing.
Iai-jutsu Sword fighting.
Isshin One heart or one mind.

Jo Japanese short staff for stick fighting.
Jodo Classical martial art of stick fighting.
Jo-jutsu Combat stick-fighting techniques.

Judo The way of gentleness or pliability, a sports-orientated form of ju-jitsu devised by Dr Jigoro Kano.
Ju-jitsu Japanese composite system of all-in fighting techniques.
Jutsu Method or technique.

Kansetsu-waza Joint-locking techniques.
Karate Generic term used to describe a variety of unarmed combat systems based on empty-handed fighting emphasising blocking and striking techniques using hands and feet. Generally acknowledged to have been brought to Japan from Okinawa by Funakoshi Gichin, founder of the original Shotokan style.
Katame-waza Holding or immobilising techniques.
Katana Japanese sword.
Kempo See *Kenpo* and *Shorinji kempo*.
Kendo The way of the sword, the *do* form of swordsmanship also practised as a sport.
Ken-jutsu Techniques of sword fighting
Kenpo Combat system derived from Chinese kung fu.
Ki The vital energy that flows around the body.
Kodokan The original school for the practice of judo founded by Jigoro Kano in 1889.
Kumi-uchi Primitive combat grappling system upon which many ju-jitsu techniques were based.

Makiwara A wooden post covered in straw used for practising striking techniques in most karate-based systems.
Mushin Empty mind.

Nage-waza Throwing techniques.
Naginata A long spear or halberd
Nunchaku A rice flail.

Sai A three-pronged, dagger-like weapon, but has no blade.

Shime-waza Strangling or choking techniques.

Shugyo Process of ascetic discipline undertaken by disciples of classical martial arts.

Shugyoka A practitioner of a martial art undergoing the process of *shugyo*.

Sumo Indigenous Japanese fighting system, now practised exclusively as a form of wrestling.

Taiho-jutsu Police combat techniques incorporating aspects of judo and ju-jitsu as well as the use of truncheons and binding methods.

Te Hand, also the name used to describe Okinawan fighting system commonly called karate.

Taekwondo Korean martial art or combat sport similar to karate emphasising high-kicking techniques in contest.

Ukemi-waza Falling techniques.

Index

Ju-Jitsu: Classical and Modern traces the history of this fascinating martial art from feudal Japan up to the present day, and explores a huge repertoire of techniques. Manoeuvres designed for every level of ability, from basic to advanced, are described and illustrated with over 200 black and white photographs and line-drawings.

Eddie Ferrie has trained extensively in a variety of martial arts, including taekwondo, karate, judo and ju-jitsu. He writes for the *Guardian*, the *Daily Mail* and *British Judo Magazine*, and is the author of *Fighting Fit*, *Taekwondo* and *Judo for Self-defence* (all published by Crowood).

- **Step-by-step instructions for both basic and advanced techniques**
- **History, philosophy and ethics of traditional ju-jitsu**
- **Practical advice on self-defence**
- **Glossary of ju-jitsu terminology**
- **Superb black and white photographs and detailed line-drawings**

ISBN 1-85223-72
ISBN 1 85223 722 8
Cover photographs by Eddie Ferrie
Cover design by Pat Warren
Printed in Great Britain

£12.99

9 781852 23722